THE SMELL

OF

MONEY

Gene Munger

ISBN: 1515149854

ISBN 13: 9781515149859

Library of Congress Control Number: 2015911889

CreateSpace Independent Publishing Platform

North Charleston, South Carolina

THIS BOOK IS DEDICATED TO MY WIFE, MOLLY. I WILL ALWAYS CHERISH HER ENCOURAGEMENT TO WRITE THIS BOOK, ALONG WITH HER INSIGHT AND CON-STRUCTIVE CRITIQUES. WITHOUT HER SUPPORT, THERE WOULD NEVER HAVE BEEN ANY OF THE FOUR BOOKS FOLLOWING MY FIRST, *MOMMA, DON'T YA WANT ME TO LEARN NOTHIN'?*

INDEED, SHE IS *THE STRAW THAT STIRS MY DRINK.*

Acknowledgments

Without the support of the following people, *The Smell of Money* would still only be an idea waiting for a computer, printer, and publisher.

CAROL NORRIS
Carol has been the initial editor on many of my past books. Her overall support has been more than significant. Her insight into organizing various story lines, editing skills, talent, patience, and commitment have continually helped make "writing like I talk" more readable and intelligible. I shall forever be indebted to her.

BETSEY BRUNER
Betsey's expertise in editing, planning, and implementing a viable and effective social media marketing plan continued at full force; it has made the difference for prior novels and helps assure successful marketing of *The Smell of Money*.

JOHN HENDERSON AND MICHAEL FRANKEL
These two special friends' continued support, encouragement, and critiques about my books always keep my mojo headed in the right direction.

SHELL OIL COMPANY'S PUBLIC AFFAIRS COLLEAGUES
Their support and wise counsel were significant during my sixteen years in Shell's Department of Public Affairs. For this book, one of my colleagues, David McKinney, a superb writer, offered me a few

draft suggestions, which were implemented in its final publishing. My continued relationship with him and my Shell colleagues is very special to me.

CREATESPACE'S EDITORS

Their helpful comments and suggestions for this book made an appreciable difference in the final publication. They were always responsive and helpful throughout the entire publishing process.

CHAPTER ONE

Lance Wilson was not a happy person. Six months earlier he had been hired as a reporter for the *Desert Breeze*, a small, biweekly newspaper in Lodi, California. It was Lance's first job at a newspaper, his first job as a reporter, and things were not going well at all.

Ralph Wiggen, the longtime editor, had hired Lance believing that this young man, a recent graduate from Chico State, had all the credentials to be a first-rate reporter. While majoring in journalism, Lance edited the school paper, the *Chico Crier*. Highly regarded by the student body, it had won honors as one of the best college newspapers in California. He was also a track star, excelling in the three-thousand-meter run, and an all-around campus leader with a résumé that cried out "Hire this guy; don't let him get away."

Regrettably, Lance's employment had been a most disappointing experience for Wiggen. His reporting required continuous rewrites, deadlines were never reached, and it didn't appear that Lance would ever come around and become any kind of a contributing reporter. Wiggen felt it was only a matter of time before this young golden boy from Chico would be terminated.

While on an early-morning run, Lance had met Ray Jackson. Ray, just out of dental school, had started his practice in Lodi only a year or so ago. Unmarried, his passion was running, and a five-mile run started his day during the week, ten miles on weekends. In the torrid summer, Ray would transfer his athleticism to the community pool, swimming laps there for at least an hour each day.

Lance liked Ray from the first meeting. He was impressed with his new friend and surprised to meet another runner in a new town. Meeting him more than relieved the loneliness he had earlier felt upon his arrival.

The *Desert Breeze* was closed on weekends. With the Friday edition put to bed late that afternoon, Lance called Ray and suggested they meet at The Office, a popular local bar where all ages, businessmen, women, yuppies, and wannabes would usually meet at week's end.

"Hey, Ray, let's meet at our favorite watering hole. It's been one helluva week for me, and I need to talk. Deal?"

"Sure, Lance, but if we can meet around six thirty, I'd appreciate it. I have a patient scheduled for four o'clock; he needs his wisdom tooth removed and is in a lot of pain. OK?"

"Yeah, that'll work. See ya then."

With Lance's boss being constantly on his case, he knew that his time with the *Breeze* was about to end. It had not been a good fit from the get-go, and he had more or less decided that before he was fired, he would quit.

As to what he would do next, he had no idea, but for sure, staying and working in Lodi was out of the question. Despite his unhappiness with his editor, his interest in journalism and making it his career was still a big part of his makeup. He had begun to feel that moving to another paper, another editor, would undoubtedly help his career plans.

Right at 6:30 p.m., Ray strolled into the bar. His appearance was eye-catching—tall, tanned, athletic, with piercing blue eyes. His presence turned heads immediately, certainly of the young women there.

Lance's earlier appearance there had also turned a few heads. Almost six feet, he walked erect and with confidence. His black, wavy hair blended nicely with his square face, pug nose, and a smile that immediately projected a friendly, approachable person.

"Over here, Ray," Lance yelled, as he stood up from the table.

Not missing a beat, Ray squeezed his way between the crowded tables, extended his long, muscular arm, and, with a firm grip, seized Lance's hand and said, "What's goin' on, bro; how ya been?"

"Hey, Ray, I'm doin' pretty good. Ya ready for a beer?"

"Boy, would I. How's about a Bud? Ya know, ya don't have to have fun to drink," Ray added with a hearty laugh that brought pleasant nods around the nearby crowded tables.

"Gotcha, man." He waved to the perky waitress heading their way. With both those men showing no wedding rings, they were what young women would call "chick magnets."

"Lance, you said you wanted to talk. Have you found some hot chick who's just dyin' to meet ya?"

"No, I haven't even found a lady here I wanted to date. It's much more serious than that. As you know, I've been working at the *Desert*

Breeze for about six months now. And to tell you the truth, I'm not happy. The editor, this guy named Wiggen, has been a colossal pain in the ass. He's never satisfied with anything I ever do. He's always bitchin' about my writing, not makin' deadlines and so on. I'll bet he's about to fire my ass. Frankly, I wanna beat him to it. I just wanna get out of there."

Ray answered quickly, "OK, bro, just what do ya wanna do? You were a journalism major. Do you wanna pursue that? Work in another newspaper? What?"

"Yes, I do, but maybe after this experience, I just might want to think about doing something else, at least for a while. You have any ideas?"

"No, not really, but if I were you, I'd start checking out the 'help wanted' ads on Google. Maybe some company might be looking for a guy with your background, your credentials. At least, I'd suggest that's a good place to start. You never know unless you try. For sure, I don't see anything in this town that would fit your pistol. Of course, the *Lodi News Sentinel* is really the only major newspaper in town, but I'm not sure they would be interested in you, especially if you leave the *Breeze* after only a few months."

"Good idea. I'll start googlin' to see if it has anything I'd be interested in. Oh, by the way, I'm driving down to LA tomorrow to get together with one of my former teammates, 'Flash' Gordon. Flash ran the sprints at Chico. Unfortunately, he tore his hamstring really bad in his senior year, and it essentially put him out of competition.

"He was a business major, landed a good job with Hughes Aircraft. I talked to him a couple of weeks ago, and he thinks that my moving to Long Beach would be a good thing. Frankly, I've never even been there, so he may be right. For sure, anything would beat my being in Lodi. At this point, I'm thinkin' that's where you go to die."

"Hey, wait a minute, Lance. Lodi's not such a bad place to live. I'm making a damned good living here as a dentist. I never thought that life would be this good, particularly since I just got out of dental school, passed the boards, and I was lucky enough to be hired by a well-established dentist here, Chuck Williams. Right after he hired me, he surprised everybody when he announced his retirement. He then offered me a deal I couldn't refuse. He wanted to sell me his business, gave me really good terms, and I now have all of his old patients. Hey, I'm one lucky dude."

"I understand, but, Ray, have you found any action in this town? Have you even had a date? Any prospects? For me, I just keep on lookin'. There must be gold in dem der hills."

Shaking his head, Ray answered, "Lance, ya gotta understand. I just don't have time right now. I'm up to my ears with my practice. Between my running and swimming, finding and dating women is simply not high on my priority list. Oh, it'll come, but I have lots of time. Lots of time."

"Gotcha. How about another beer? It's Friday. We deserve it!"

CHAPTER TWO

After a few more beers and a double cheeseburger at The Office, Lance drove back to his apartment, a relatively modern two-story building located just east of Lodi's downtown. Ray's idea to check out Google for employment opportunities had possibilities. Musing, he figured he could do that when he visited Flash this weekend. Maybe some company would need a staff writer to do their publications. Maybe, too, he could get a job as a public-relations guy. He knew he didn't know a whole lot about public relations, but he had had an introductory course at Chico. He had aced it and was confident that he could talk his way into that kind of work. Whatever, he knew he needed to make a change in his life.

Heeding Ray's advice, he googled the help-wanted Internet postings for journalists. Nothing was available, but he did find that an oil refinery in the Long Beach area was looking for a public-relations manager. He knew his résumé would probably not attract a lot of interest, but, as a student, he had volunteered in his junior and senior years for a Chico's food bank and did their public relations, a position he received many accolades for. If he could be selected for an interview, he believed he could sell himself for the job. At least it was a start; he'd look into it later.

Before he went to bed, he searched MapQuest to determine how to get to Long Beach to find Flash's place. From Lodi, it was going to take about six hours. If he left early in the morning to cruise down I-5, he could easily rendezvous with Flash around noon. A good idea, he thought. He couldn't wait to start this adventure.

This route was unfamiliar to him, one which he had never driven. Behind the wheel of his 2003 Highlander, it certainly wasn't a meandering journey through verdant meadows and picturesque scenery, but the highway, absent stop signs and local businesses, made for a straightforward ride to Long Beach.

Lance called Flash as he moved from I-5 to the San Diego Freeway, I-405. Excited, Flash gave him specific directions to his condo, about forty minutes away.

"Lance, you're really going to like this area—the beach, great restaurants, and I might add, many, many lovely ladies, damsels in distress needing a man's strong arm and a generous bank account to get them through the evening."

Laughing at his friend's humorous comments, Lance said, "OK, Flash, I'm their man—credentials in hand and ready to rumble. I can't wait to see you."

As Lance arrived, he could see Flash yelling down from his upstairs veranda, beer in hand and giving a loud, "Hi ya, dude, welcome to paradise. Park that heap and come on up!"

His condo was everything Lance thought Long Beach would be—first-class landscape, well-designed buildings, swimming pool, and exercise room—a far cry from his digs in Lodi.

As Lance walked up, he jabbered all the way to the condo. "I'll tell you what; you sure are in "high society". I bet you told the guy who sold you this jewel that you were a world-class track man. Right?"

Flash laughed and responded in a semiserious manner, "Naww, Lance, those days are behind me now. I've got a really good job with Hughes, working with their marketing group—great guys—helpful and supportive. I'm really happy. I got lucky, knowing how slow the job market was when we graduated. How about you? As I recall, you're working for a newspaper up in Lodi. Are you happy with it?"

"No, not really. I'm about to blow out of there. I hate my boss. Lodi's a hick town, and I'm looking to change, sooner rather than later."

"Gee, Lance, I'm sorry. Whadda ya have in mind doin'? Workin' for another newspaper? What?"

"Well, I have this friend in Lodi who suggested that I google the help-wanted postings and see what's cookin'. I did…found almost no one looking for a reporter, a journalist, but one I saw caught my eye. It's a refinery just east of Long Beach, the Bellflower Refinery, located in Bellflower. It's a small town, less than thirty-five hundred residents, and they're looking for a public-relations manager."

Flash's face turned dour, and he said, "What? A public-relations man for an oil refinery? You have got to be kidding. Why in the world would you ever want to work there? First, everybody who drives by that place complains about the smell, even those on the 405. Come on, Lance, you're a journalist, a reporter, not a PR man. You don't know anything about public relations. Can you imagine trying to put on a good face for a refinery that smells, has fires, drops toxic chemicals all over the neighborhood, schools, whatever? You've got to be out of your mind."

"Yeah, I know, but at least I can check it out."

"Now that I think about it, Lance, that refinery has been looking for a flack for the last three months. They fired the last one there. No wonder they're still looking for his replacement. No one wants to work there."

Hearing Flash's damning words caused Lance to think maybe he shouldn't even consider sending the refinery a résumé, but if he was going to leave the *Desert Breeze,* he had to do that soonest. He had had enough of the place, enough of the town.

After making his point, Flash moved on and said, "Let's go now and hit the happy hour at my favorite watering hole, Pacific Wave. Lance, you're really gonna like it. It has good bar food, lively band, dance floor, and always a bevy of really hot chicks. One thing about Southern California girls, they are much more advanced than Chico State's girls—by a long stretch."

"Sounds like you've found a home there, Flash, but have you found any special girl, anyone you're dating steady?"

"Oh, heavens no, I'm just playing the field. I just don't have time to get serious at this stage. The job at Hughes is priority. Getting serious will come later."

"OK, I understand, Flash, but I'm really not too comfortable going to a place like the Pacific Wave. You say it's really hoppin', but that sort of intimidates me. I much prefer quieter places where I can talk to women without all that bar-hopping noise."

"Oh, come now, Lance. You're not in your eighties. Lighten up. Live a little. Who knows, you might get lucky and score. Come on, let's roll. I know you're going to like it."

"Well, Flash, I hate to admit it, but I'm a virgin. I've never done that with a girl. Never. Yeah, Rachael and I went steady for a while at Chico, but neither one of us ever wanted to have sex; we were both afraid that she would get pregnant. It was never an issue. It was just the way it was."

"Yikes, I understand, but Lance, we're in the twenty-first century. This isn't the Victorian age. Come on, lighten up, bro."

Knowing that his confession to Flash was a complete surprise to his friend, he regretted it. He'd just have to go along with Flash, playacting that he was one hip guy looking to have a little fun, going with the flow.

Entering the Wave was exactly what Flash had described. The place was crowded, the band was rollin' hot and heavy, and the dance floor was crowded, even girls dancing with girls. The drinking from all tables was moving at Mach speed; waitresses couldn't fill the orders and refills fast enough. Indeed, this was the place. Lance tried to smile, looking like he was happy to be there and just one of the guys. But deep in his gut, he almost wished he was back at Chico with Rachael.

There were no tables available, so Flash led them to the bar. Lance ordered a beer, Flash a margarita. Served, they swerved around in their chairs and watched the frenetic action on the Royce floor. It was intoxicating, even to Lance. He was beginning to enjoy himself.

About that time, two very attractive ladies—blondes, long hair, svelte bodies, and engaging smiles—approached the two and asked if they would like to dance. Flash couldn't get up from the stool fast enough. "You betcha. Let's go."

The other, even more dazzling than the first, asked, "How about you, fella; wanna dance?"

Looking down and not really facing the lady, Lance replied meekly, "Err, I, err, don't dance very well, I, uh."

"Well then, let's talk." She gracefully directed her hand to him. "My name is Libby. What's your name?"

"Uh, my name is Lance. Lance Wilson. Glad to meet you."

"Are you new in town? I don't think I've ever seen you here before. Did you just move here, or just passing through?"

"No, I live in Lodi. I'm here visiting my friend—that's the guy your friend is dancing with."

"Lodi? Why in the world are you living in that place? You gotta move here. As someone once said, don't remember who, there's no there there." Libby laughed heartily at that remark.

"Well, I'm thinking about it, but I haven't found a job yet."

"What can you bring to the party, Lance? What kind of job are you looking for?"

"I work for a newspaper there; I'm a reporter. I thought I might find a job at a newspaper here. Do you have any suggestions?"

"Well, I know the *LA Times*. The *Long Beach Press Telegram* is the other one I'm familiar with, but that's about it. Right now, I'm a waitress at Denny's. The tips aren't bad, either. Look, Lance, all I wanna do right now is have some fun, have a party—you know, get down, baby, get down."

Lance blinked at her freshness, her candor, but he could see there was absolutely no future intellectual relationship with her. "Great, Libby, may I buy you a drink?"

"I'd love one. Extra-dry Beefeaters martini—two olives, straight up." Lance gulped at her order; he had never even had a martini. She seemed to be very well acquainted with it. He felt "gapped."

As Libby was served, she suddenly raised her hand and yelled, "Hey, Ralph, here I am. I'll be there in a minute."

Lance looked across the room, turned to Libby, and said, "Gee, that must be your date?"

"Yes, it is. I'd ask him over to meet you, but it's best that not happen. He tends to be a little jealous. Seeing me with you would not make him happy." Nestling her martini next to her willowy hip, she made her move and said, "Nice meeting you, Lance; thanks for the drink. Maybe I'll be seeing you again sometime." With that, she moved quickly across the room and greeted her date with a long, lingering kiss, and the two immediately left the building.

Lance sat there stunned. He mused as he thought, *If this is the kind of girl I'm going to meet here in Long Beach, I'd better stay in Lodi. This is no place for me.*

About that time, Flash was leaving the dance floor, but without the lady he had just met. He said in a disappointed voice, "Sometimes you can't win for losing. That chick just abruptly left me on the floor. Said something about she needed to see this guy who had just sat down at one of the tables. I didn't ask any questions. I guess that's just the way it sometimes goes around here. Ready to go back to my place? I'm ready."

Driving home, Lance asked, "Flash, I've never quite had an experience like the one I had back there. This other girl and I had just started getting acquainted, I bought her a drink, and then, bam, she spotted this guy across the room—her date, she said—and left me thinking I must have bad breath."

"Think nothing of it, Lance. That's the way it is around here. These ladies survey us men quickly, make a decision as to whether or not they want to spend any quality time, and if not, they'll leave you in a New York minute. So forget it."

Lance didn't respond. Instead, he just sat there in the car and tried to review what had happened. Yes, living in Long Beach had already presented some things that not only were new to him, but downright weird. He truly needed an education.

CHAPTER THREE

L ance continued to be disturbed hearing Flash's negative tirade against the Bellflower Refinery. He had never been associated with a refinery—the downbeat attitudes of the surrounding neighbors, motorists driving by it. He was raised in Sacramento, and the nearest refineries were in Martinez and Benicia, about one hundred miles south. Prior to driving to Long Beach, he had googled the refinery to review its profile.

Being ignorant about any refineries in general, he found Bellflower was more than a minor player as a refinery. It was pretty impressive. Wikipedia came to his rescue.

In operation since the mid-1920s, it currently had a total crude-oil capacity of about one hundred thousand barrels per day, primarily supplying gasoline, jet fuel, and diesel fuel to markets in Southern California. It got its crude oil via pipeline from Canada, by rail from the central United States, and by tankers from Alaska.

Bellflower even had a retail-marketing system that included about fifteen hundred stations, selling the nonmajor brand called Jet. Its corporate headquarters were located in Denver.

Lance was pleased with that information. He hadn't divulged it to Flash, but Bellflower appeared to be a successful operation. He now needed to accumulate more information as to its reputation in the area. The Bellflower Chamber of Commerce would probably be able to give him that information.

Leaving Flash and before starting the trek back to Lodi, he called the chamber and identified himself as a resident of Bend, Oregon, who was interested in moving to the area. The chamber's female associate, Linda Langston, very pleasant and enthusiastic, responded to Lance and said, "This is a lovely place to live—close to beaches, not too far from Disneyland, good schools, and good neighborhoods."

Lance quickly asked, "Yes, but I've heard there's a refinery near there. What is its reputation? Is it a good neighbor? I just drove by there, and neighborhoods literally surround it. How do the two get along?"

"Oh, my, just fine. No problems there," she said. "Many of the neighbors work there, and, of course, they're sort of the disciples, explaining to their neighbors what's going on there. I've really heard nothing bad about the refinery; it and their neighbors seem to get along just fine."

CHAPTER FOUR

D riving back to Lodi gave Lance time to think about his next move—should he send his résumé to Bellflower or not? He remained puzzled after hearing the chamber's glowing report of the refinery's excellent reputation. He questioned how that could be, for an oil refinery is generally known for its pollution, noise, and so on. He could do house-to-house interviews posing as a representative for a public-relations firm. He'd never done such a thing, but he didn't think it would be too difficult to pull off—something to think about.

Back in Lodi, he dusted off his initial résumé, filled in his latest employment with the *Breeze*, and began to draft his response to Bellflower's "help-wanted" request for a public-relations director. He knew he'd have to list his editor, Ralph Wiggen, as a reference. Whether that would result in a positive recommendation remained to be seen.

Lance decided he would have to start schmoozing his boss, substantially improving his reporting, and falsely suggesting that the job change was a result of his fiancée now living in the Long Beach area and her insistence that they get married as soon as possible. That sounded like a plausible approach, one that should be reasonable and understandable to the boss.

Starting Monday, he began to implement his plan, sending the résumé and "sucking up" to the editor. At first, Wiggen was overwhelmed by his fledging reporter's attitude change, positive and helpful. In a few days, his attitude toward his young reporter improved enormously.

After not hearing from Bellflower for almost two weeks, paranoia set in big time. He felt the lack of response and disinterest was because of his lack of experience in the field of public relations. That could be, but Lance was confident that if he only could get an interview, his personality and charm would carry the day. It always had, and there was no reason it couldn't for the PR position.

Lance finally heard from Bellflower. Literally ripping open the envelope, he quickly scanned the positive words carefully presented on the first page: "We would like to schedule an interview with you at your earliest convenience. Please contact our Human Relations Manager, Sonia Thomas, for an appointment. We look forward hearing from you."

Those were flattering words—maybe they were serious; maybe they really wanted him to work for them. Before he would respond, he dropped in on his editor and told him about the interview and why he was pursuing it. Wiggen took the bait completely and said he would be delighted to give him a favorable reference.

Lance called Ms. Thomas and stated that if convenient to her, he could be in Bellflower that Friday. She responded in a most pleasant and enthusiastic voice, "That would be just fine, Lance. If you wish, you could come down on Thursday evening; accommodations would be at the Holiday Inn just off the I-405 interchange in Bellflower." She would arrange to have breakfast with him the next morning at 8:00 a.m. and then take him to the refinery to start the interviews.

Lance was ecstatic with the plan, staying at a Holiday Inn—the refinery paying for it was a bonus; to him, that was first-class. It was also a long way from the reception he had received with Wiggen when he came to Lodi for his interview. They had coffee at the editor's desk, and Wiggen offered to pay him the generous sum of $600 a month with the promise of a raise after a successful probationary period of six months. Fresh out of college, he needed the job and the money.

He knew his Toyota Highlander's well-worn tires were more than suspect for another trip to Bellflower, so he took a deep breath and looked at the balance on his Visa credit card, knowing in another hundred dollars, he would be over his credit limit. He went to Oscar's, a well-known used car and tire store, and bargained to buy two tires. Gazing sadly at the other two tires, Oscar urged him to buy those, too. Lance hemmed and hawed, bought only two tires, and prepared to leave the next day at noon.

Lance's wardrobe was minimal; he had only a sport coat, khaki pants, one white shirt, a Chico State tie, and shoes that hadn't seen any sign of polish in more than a year. This freaked him a little, but with his cash reserve at almost nothing, he relaxed and thought, *Well, if they really want to hire me, they'll have to take me as I am, not as they might want me to be.*

He tossed and turned throughout the night. Sleep was sporadic. Not even waiting to hear his alarm, he bounded out of bed at 4:30 a.m., an hour he'd never before experienced. Pulling himself together, he watched a little TV and called his parents and Ray, his Lodi running partner, to tell them about his immediate plans. His parents were pleased for him. Ray wished him well and did not mention his previous doubts about Lance taking a public-relations job.

Lance felt he was on his way to perhaps change his life, certainly his lifestyle. First, he had to convince his potential employer that he was the man for the job. His confidence had never been higher.

CHAPTER FIVE

L ance arrived at the Holiday Inn late in the afternoon. Motoring down the interstate, he was filled with anticipation of his interview the next morning. He would practice his presentation, talking to himself and thinking about other questions he would be asked. He had never met Ms. Thomas, but the earlier conversation they had had was pleasant and encouraging. Whatever, he would be ready.

Excited about the impending interview, he decided to drive around Bellflower and take a look at the refinery, a mass of towers, pipes, and equipment. A short drive west had him at the Pacific Ocean. He parked his SUV and watched the sunset over the endless expanse of ocean. He had never had this experience; he never knew how special it could be.

A good night's rest at the Holiday Inn more than prepared him for the day to come; he was fired up and ready to go. Lance waited for his room's phone to ring. It came precisely at 8:00 a.m.

He answered promptly and said, "Hello, Lance Wilson speaking."

"Good morning, Lance. This is Sonia Thomas. 'Bout ready for breakfast?"

Eagerly he replied, "Yes, thank you, Ms. Thomas, I am. Shall I meet you in the lobby?"

"That's fine. I'll be waiting for you. I'll have on a blue pants suit and a checkered blouse. It should be easy for you to spot me."

Seeing her for the first time mirrored exactly what he had thought she would look like: middle-aged, stylishly dressed but not overly, pleasing smile, and touches of gray slowly beginning to creep on the side of her well-groomed hair. He had never met a human-resource person, but in his view, she met all of his expectations.

After exchanging a few pleasantries, they ordered, and the questions started, first with the usual: "Tell me about yourself."

Lance was ready for that one. In a plain, no-frills response, he reviewed his life—growing up in Sacramento, going to Chico State, his athletic and leadership accomplishments, and particularly his public-relations experience with the food bank. She smiled and nodded throughout his review; he could see she was impressed.

"Now, let me tell you about the job you are seeking, Lance. You will be looked upon as the conscience of the refinery. You will be our primary spokesperson, our primary liaison to the neighborhood, Chamber of Commerce, city council, and especially the media. It'll be challenging, but I wouldn't be here talking to you if I didn't think you were a viable candidate. Bellflower is looking for the best person for the job. Why do you think you're the one? I see you have minimal public-relations experience; you've only been a newspaper reporter. Are you the pro we're looking for?"

Lance was ready for that question and had practiced his response many times over. Leaning forward in his chair, eyes focused on his interviewer, he made his case.

"Ms. Thomas, as my résumé indicated, I'm a journalist. I was Chico State's school's newspaper editor for two years, a position that required me to deal continuously with journalism students. From experience, I learned to finesse them, to work around their egos, help them develop their skills—in a word, create a partnership with them. We won two, not one, awards as the best university newspaper on the West Coast, ranking above the big ones—USC, UCLA, even Stanford. I must say it was not all about me; it was about us, our team. That experience, what I've learned, can be transferred as your public-relations man here at Bellflower.

"I also was a middle-distance runner on the track-and-field team. In our conference, I was its three-thousand-meter champion in my senior year; I anchored the four-thousand-meter relay team, also the conference champion. Running track and field is not an individual sport; it takes teammates, relationships, believing in your coaches. I'm very proud of my record there. I'm a leader, Ms. Thomas, a born leader, and that leadership will transfer to the refinery. I'll be the best public-relations man you've ever seen."

Lance frankly couldn't believe how impressive those words had been; he had even overwhelmed himself with them. Easing back in the chair, he waited for her response.

"Well, Lance, I must say that was really something. You really believe you're the man for the job. Now, your next step this morning is to meet and talk to some of the refinery's process and health-and-safety managers. They have your résumé and will be anxious to talk to you. Let's drive over, meet them, and get on with your interviews. The last person you'll be talking to is the refinery manager; his name is Jess Peterson. He's known here as 'Pete.' He's been here for the past ten years and is what you might call a legend before his time. He's anxious to meet you."

As they were driving back to the refinery, Lance asked, "Oh, by the way, Ms. Thomas…"

"Lance, please call me Sonia. We all are on a first-name basis around here. You'll never hear mister or missus or miss. Never. OK?"

"Right, it's just the way I was raised." The question he wanted to ask was "What's the salary?" Driving through the gate, the acrid odor of petroleum filled the air. He had heard about those odors, but smelling it the first time, so close, it was really offensive. He decided not to press it. That could come later.

For the rest of the morning and into the midafternoon, Lance went through the ritual of meeting and talking with the other refinery managers. Their offices were not elaborate at all. It was obvious there was no need for any excessive trappings. Work was paramount there, no time for anything else.

In interview after interview, Lance repeated his standard "elevator speech," which appeared to go well with all of them. One of the process managers asked, "Do you have a mechanical aptitude?"

Before he answered that question, he paused and thought about his answer, knowing full well he honestly had none. Screwdrivers, pliers, and even wrenches were a challenge to him. "Yes, I believe I have; however, I'll look to you and others to brief me on the manufacturing processes of these units, how gasoline and diesel oil are processed. I'm a quick learner, but I'll need your help." That response appeared to be satisfactory. To his relief, that question was never asked again.

The penulimate interview was with the health-and-safety manager. To his surprise, safety was not just a word; it was one of the refinery's primary focuses. The manager continuously emphasized how important it was in day-to-day operations. A "lost-time accident" was like a visit from Darth Vader. As he found out later, the refinery's safety record was not that great—good, maybe, but certainly not great.

Sonia waited outside the manager's door for the interview to end. She greeted Lance and took him over to meet Jess Peterson, the refinery manager. As Lance discovered, while he wasn't a deity, he was certainly considered to be close to it.

Entering the man's office, accompanied by Sonia, Lance was impressed with its JFK-like oak desk, a rich, leather-padded swivel chair, pictures of his family, previous refinery honors, and a picture of him and President George W. Bush shaking hands.

Pete rose quickly from his chair and made a swift move around the desk to meet Lance, shook his hand mightily, and welcomed him warmly. He was not a remarkably striking or handsome man. About five feet eight in height, his tanned face was clear of either a moustache or beard. As he smiled with a mouthful of uneven teeth, it looked like he hadn't brushed them in a long time. It could have been his smoking, although his office had no stale smell of tobacco.

"Nice to meet you, Lance, and welcome to Bellflower. Please sit down." His deep, resonant voice filled the room nicely. He was obviously in control in his kingdom. "I've seen your résumé and have been looking forward to meeting you."

"Pleased to be here, Mr. Peterson, and…"

"Whoa, wait a minute, Lance. Mr. Peterson left us a long time ago. My name is Pete. OK? Tell me, what interests you about this job?"

"Yes sir, Pete. I understand."

Predicting what the man would ask next, Lance preempted the question and repeated his well-rehearsed response, stating almost word-for-word what he had recited to Sonia. Before Pete could ask the next question, Lance made the positive point that while he had a minimum of actual public-relations experience, his background as a newspaper editor and athlete made him qualified for the position. Further, he was an accomplished writer, a talent that he knew would be necessary in the position.

Pete did not appear comfortable with Lance's rapid-fire response to a question that he wanted to ask; however, those were exactly the answers he wanted to hear. That impressed him; he already liked the young man's style, but his youth and lack of knowledge about refinery operations concerned him. However, he was confident that Lance's limited knowledge could be greatly expanded over time. He was certainly "teachable."

Before Lance spoke again, Sonia filled the void and said, "Lance, you haven't asked, but the position we're looking for you to fill, we believe should be attractive to you. The starting annual salary is fifty-five thousand dollars, complete health care, expense account, and two weeks' vacation after one year, three weeks after three years, a company car, fully maintained, and a full-time secretary. All in all, we think it's a pretty liberal package."

Lance smiled before answering and thought, "Good gracious, almighty. Here I am making peanuts over in Lodi, living hand-to-mouth, driving an old, weather-beaten car, no expense account, no health care. I must be dreaming."

He finally answered and with a beaming smile said, "Yes, Sonia, that's a very liberal package. I guess my next question is, when do I start?"

Both Pete and Sonia laughed energetically at that question. She answered, "Well, you see, we have three more applicants for the position. Of course, we will be checking your references. We should be able to make a decision in a few days. Stand by. We'll let you know. Thank you for being here, Lance; it has been a pleasure to meet you.

By the way, those other process managers who met you were very pleased; they liked you very much."

Lance wanted to get Pete's view on public relations, but he figured that would come later. He was more than pleased with the interview and proudly announced, "Thank you, both of you. I thoroughly enjoyed being here. I look forward to hearing favorably from you. If I'm given the chance, I believe I'll really like working here."

As Lance prepared to leave, Pete accompanied them to the door and into the parking lot and Sonia's car. While waiting to join Sonia in her car, Lance stopped, turned to the refinery manager, and naively said, "Pete, I guess it's the petroleum odor I smell coming from the refinery. Is it?"

"Yes, Lance," he answered with a broad smile on his tanned face. "It is, and that's the smell of money."

CHAPTER SIX

Lance neither acknowledged nor commented about what he had just heard. Further, he had no idea how Pete felt about the refinery's public relations. He hoped that Pete would be encouraging, but the smell of money? That disturbed him. Yes, he wanted the job, but did he want to be working at a place that smelled like oil, gasoline, diesel fuel? Maybe Flash was right. He had to be out of his mind to even think of such a move. He'd have to think about it should he be offered the job. Yes, he'd really have to think about it.

Lance considered calling Flash, but there would be no question about what he would say: "Yeah, Lance, as I told you a few weeks ago, don't even think about going to work for an oil refinery. You're much better than that. Stick to journalism. Get a job at a newspaper, whatever, but do not change directions and start working for a refinery." Lance certainly didn't need to hear that; he'd just avoid his friend and wait to see if an offer was made.

Reflecting further, Lance was overwhelmed with the offer Bellflower had given him. Hell, he was just out of college. He was barely able to live on what he was making at the *Desert Breeze*. With Bellflower's salary, benefits, company car, and expense account, he'd know he had finally arrived. He would be in "high society". Yes, the odor bothered him, but maybe he'd get used to it, actually like the job, and move on from there. He could always try it, and if he didn't like it, he'd resign. No harm, no foul.

Actually, despite his misgivings about working at the *Breeze*, he really liked journalism and the challenge of reporting, interviewing newsmakers, and writing editorials. Perhaps, he should forego becoming a public-relations man and pursue finding a job at another paper. That was what his education and experience at Chico had prepared him for—certainly not for public relations, especially at a refinery.

A week passed. No word from Sonia. Maybe they had found someone else for the job, a person who was imminently more qualified than he was. Maybe his editor didn't give him a good reference. He'd given it his best shot; he'd just have to wait.

Back at the *Breeze*, Lance was busy reporting on a developer's plan to build a plant to manufacture power lawn mowers. He had covered the developer from the initial press release, which, when delivered to the *Breeze*, produced a scoop that spread like wildflower in the area. Wiggen praised him so much that Lance felt again that newspaper reporting was actually where he wanted to be. That got his reporting juices flowing heavily; he was on fire again.

Lance liked the company's spokesperson, Toby Littleton. With his explanation, Lance developed a reasonable understanding of the process, zoning changes, permits, and all the details that needed to be in hand before actual construction would start.

Around three o'clock on a Friday afternoon, Lance's cell phone, on vibrate, broke his train of thought about drafting an article on a company located in Lodi that would employ at least fifty good-paying jobs. Glancing at the caller ID, his heart raced quickly and his palms became sweaty. He got out of his chair and departed to just outside the building.

"Hello there, this is Lance Wilson. How may I help you?"

"Hi, Lance, this is Sonia Thomas, the same Sonia who is about to offer you a job at the Bellflower Refinery. How are you today?"

"Well, hi, Sonia, I've been waiting for your call. You're offering me a job?" His lack of enthusiasm and timid response belied his true feeling about finally hearing from Sonia.

"That's exactly why I'm calling. We want you at our plant. We believe you'll be the best public-relations man we've ever had there. What say you, Mr. Wilson? Are you ready to become part of our team?"

Lance took a deep breath, reflected on his recent thoughts about staying as a reporter versus the bountiful offer made to him, and answered strongly, "Well, I have to be honest with you. I've done a lot of thinking about refusing your offer and continuing to be a reporter, but working at Bellflower will be a challenge, and I'm more than ready to give it a whirl. I say, when do I go to work? I'm ready to start yesterday. Can you fix that?" His good-humored response, which had made him well liked at Chico, had been resurrected in grand style.

"Outstanding, Lance, we'd like you to report on Monday, June 1. We figure that it's going to take a few weeks to get your act together there, leave the newspaper, say good-bye to your friends, find a place to live over here—all the details one goes through when moving. And, oh yes, another good thing—Bellflower will move you at its cost, and wherever you rent, your security deposit as well as your first month's rent will be paid."

Sonia continued, "I'm not sure if you'll be in a position to buy a place, but if you do, they'll pay all closing costs associated with the sale. The point is, Lance, moving can be expensive. We want to make your move as stress-free as we can, with no undue strain on your finances. Any questions?"

"No questions from here. I more than appreciate that, Sonia. It's a great relief to have the moving costs covered. Look for me to report on June 1. I'll be ready to go."

Coming back inside feeling very excited to hear about his new job, Lance noticed that Wiggen was in his office talking to someone on the phone. Knowing his boss relatively well at this stage, he knew the conversation he was watching was strictly business. The editor's face maintained a contentious scowl; his right hand's fingers kept rat-a-tat-tatting on the top of his messy steel desk. His round head kept rotating back and forth, showing he was not impressed by the person with whom he was talking. Lance felt maybe he should break the news about his leaving in the morning. Then again, he didn't want to postpone it; he had many things to do, starting with giving a two-week notice. He was leaving. A half hour passed; when would his boss get off the damn phone?

As Lance was about to leave, Wiggen stormed out of his office, bellowing as if he had just been T-boned by a two-ton truck. "You wouldn't believe the conversation I just had with my boss. He's blaming me for the lack of circulation, poor advertising revenue, not being aware of what's goin' on in this town. I let the sumbitch rant and rave and then spent the last fifteen minutes defending us, telling him what we've been doing, getting the scoop on the new manufacturing plant, telling him how good you are doing. I think he did cool down, but hell's fire, I've forgotten more about the news business than this young punk will ever know."

Lance made no comment, knowing then that he would break the news to his boss the next morning. Doing it now could practically cause a tsunami in the desert around Lodi.

CHAPTER SEVEN

Wiggen always started his workday at five o'clock in the morning. Knowing that, Lance decided that breaking the news at that hour would be the best way to avoid any unnecessary ill feelings. Hopefully, it would be a comfortable conversation. It was puzzling that his editor had made no mention of receiving an inquiry or a reference from the refinery. Maybe the refinery hadn't even sent him one. If that were the case, telling his boss that he was leaving wouldn't necessarily make his day. Lance feared the prospect of a nasty confrontation but hoped for the best.

Lance came into his editor's office the next morning and said, "Good mornin', Ralph, I need to talk to you."

Wiggen looked up with a face of amazement. "Am I dreamin' or something, or is that really you, Lance? I've never seen you here this early. What's up?"

"I hate to tell you this, but I'm leaving the *Breeze* and taking another job." Wiggen's eyebrows looked like they were going to lift right off his round face. His arms extended wide across his broad chest as he arose from his swivel chair and said in a totally disbelieving voice, "You're going to do what?"

"I'm taking a job as the public-relations director at the Bellflower Refinery, the one I told you about a few weeks ago."

"Oh, yeah, I remember now. I do remember. Frankly, I felt that due to your lack of public-relations experience, they'd pass you by, but I had lots of faith in you." His face brightened as he said, "Well, congratulations, Lance. They'll be getting a really good man."

Lance obviously was pleased with his boss's kind words. Schmoozing him over the past few weeks had paid off. His boss was totally on board, completely devoid of ill feelings.

The air was cleared for a fun exchange as Wiggen asked, "By the way, when do they want you to start, and hold it, where in the hell is the Bellflower Refinery? Saudi Arabia? Where?"

"No, it's next to Long Beach. They want me to start there on June 1."

"Hey, Lance, we can make that work," Wiggen said. "I had kind of felt that you would be taking that job if they offered it to you, so I've lined up a guy who just moved here from Stockton, an experienced reporter who worked for the *Stockton Record*. As you know, we've got a hot story working around here—new plant, lots of jobs. We'll miss you, but we won't miss a beat keeping all the news current."

"Ralph, I didn't make up my mind until yesterday. It was a hard decision for me to make. I really have enjoyed working here, but their offer was just too good to turn down." By now, Lance was ahead of the game. His boss was happy, and he was happy. A win-win for both of them.

He thought about calling Sonia and suggesting he could start sooner than June 1, but he needed to clear his head, get out of his apartment, move his stuff, rent a new place down there, and be in a position to hit the ground running. Time, for the present, was definitely in his favor.

CHAPTER EIGHT

The decision to stick to his June 1 start date was a good one. Moving and finding a place in Long Beach, as well as visiting Ikea and a multitude of used-furniture stores, took more time than he had planned. His place now looked like a nifty bachelor's pad; he was more than pleased with the outcome. Lance thought some entertaining was a definite possibility.

With a clear head, relaxed and fully settled into his new apartment, Lance reported to Bellflower, right on schedule and on time. He was greeted cordially and spent most of the morning reviewing and signing the usual forms for a new employee. His office was a far cry from his cubbyhole at the *Breeze*. This was the real thing: spacious, modern desk, file cabinets, iPhone, and even a window facing one of the units in the distance. He met his secretary, Monica Moore—tall and strikingly attractive, fashionably dressed, with a six-year employment record ranked as a "five," the refinery's highest administrative rating.

Her tone was very professional: "Mr. Wilson, I am pleased to be your secretary. Please call on me should you have any questions." Then, in a reversal of her formal greetings, she laughingly said, "And by the way, I don't know where all the bodies are around here, but I sure do know where most of them are."

"Well, thank you, Monica, but please call me Lance. OK? I really appreciate your experience here. You will be invaluable to me."

"Thank you, Lance. Now it's time for me to take you over to maintenance to meet Bull Talbot. He's the manager, and he'll show you your company car. Bull has been around here a long time, some think too long, but when you get to know him, you'll like him. Ready to go?"

"Yes, ma'am. Let's do it. I presume it won't be a Rolls-Royce, will it? That's my personal car."

"No, no Rolls, but I guess a Ferrari will work?"

"Yeah, I guess so, at least for the time being." He loved their conversation and the good humor; they were going to get along just fine.

Meeting Bull was exactly what he had expected. He was definitely a "bull" of a man, with a slight paunch, crew cut, and graying hair. Lance had never met a maintenance man, but his welcoming grip nearly brought Lance to his knees—certainly no man to mess with.

Their initial meeting was not that cordial. Bull looked at the new kid on the block suspiciously. Lance knew it would take some time to gain his favor.

"Hey, Mr. Wilson, I want you to know I've been around here for a long time. I've seen folks like you come and go. I sure as hell hope you know what you're doing, 'cause the last PR man here didn't know his butt from nothin'. And I'll be watchin' you; we all will. You also need to know that ole Pete and I are good friends. We've drunk a lot of beer together, so if you ain't cuttin' it, he'll lemme know."

Lance blinked quickly, already intimidated. A maintenance manager who was a buddy with the refinery manager? Staying on the good side of Bull would be necessary, but he hoped he would not have to be all that involved with him.

Lance replied with false bravado, "Well, Bull, I trust you won't have to worry about what I do here. I think we'll all have to work together. One man can't do it all, especially in dealing with the public and the media. So, I'll do what I can to help you, and anything you can do to make my job easier will be appreciated. OK?"

"Yeah, I'll remember that. Now, lemme show you your company car. It's a Ford Fusion. Has hardly been driven, almost brand new. We take care of its maintenance, so don't hesitate to bring it over if anything goes wrong."

"Got it, Bull, and nice meeting you. Thanks for making arrangements for the Fusion."

CHAPTER NINE

After meeting Bull, Lance began to wonder whether a refinery was going to be a pleasant place to work. He was taken aback by the maintenance manager's demeaning attitude about his predecessor. He had never met the man, but no negative comments had been passed on to him. When Lance asked, "What happened to the former PR man?" Sonia casually responded that he had left for personal reasons. That wasn't important information to Lance; he couldn't worry about what his predecessor had or hadn't done. He knew what had to be done, and he was ready to do just that.

His first day ended with no further meetings. He and Monica worked out a schedule with the superintendent and the various process managers. Additionally, she gave him the names of the mayor and city council and the Chamber of Commerce's president. He would eventually meet them all, but his first priority was to become acquainted with the refinery's basic operations and its managers.

When Lance arrived the next morning, Monica greeted him with a hot cup of coffee in her hand. "Mornin', Lance, I presume you like your coffee black?"

"Yes, thank you, Monica. That would work well." He laughed to himself, thinking he had never had his first cup of coffee presented to him by a secretary, or anyone else. He definitely could get used to that.

"Looking at my schedule today, I see my first meeting is with the superintendent; his name is Jared DeWitt; he's referred to as 'J. B.' I met him during the interviews. He seemed to be a good man."

"Oh, yes. You'll like JB. Has been here for at least twelve years, longer than Pete. Lemme take you over to his office."

DeWitt's office was right across from the main building. Meeting Lance again, he congratulated him, wishing him well and advising that he would be available to help him any way he could. Lance liked the man's affable personality; he believed he would have a close ally as he set about to develop a strategy and implement a public-relations plan. He had never specifically done that before, but his training as Chico State's newspaper's editor had shown him how necessary it is to have a well-organized operation.

JB gave a broad review of the various processing units, speaking mostly in layman's terms that could be understood even by a teenager. Lance sorely needed that, since his mechanical aptitude was rather limited. With units like a hydrotreater, catalytic cracker, and desalter, he realized he was entering a realm of machines and equipment far removed from press releases and split infinitives.

"JB, what happens when the crude oil comes to Bellflower? How do they make gasoline and diesel fuel? I apologize for my ignorance, but I just don't know how it's done."

"Lance, those aren't stupid questions. Lemme explain it to you in really simple terms. The crude we receive is first washed at the desalter unit, where the salt is removed. Then it enters the distillation unit that distills the crude oil into fractions. The lighter fractions of the crude rise to the top, like gasoline, and the lower elements go to the bottom and require more heat, like diesel fuel and so on. That's about it. Here's a book that explains how refined products are made from crude oil. You'll want to read it, and anything you don't understand, lemme know. Believe me; we have lots of guys around here who can explain it even better than I."

As the session ended, Lance asked JB a question he and his friends had asked many times: "Why was the gasoline at companies like Chevron and BP always priced higher, a lot higher, than, for instance, QTs? Is their gasoline that much better?"

JB laughed heartily, got up from his desk, and said, "Well, Lance, that is one of the myths that the majors have been pulling over our eyes for years. No, there's no difference at all. It's all the same. Same with diesel fuel. It's all the same.

"The gasoline we process here is sold under the Jet brand at our stations. Yes, we can sell it for much lower than the majors. Our customers are the winners. They like our gasoline. It's just as good as theirs. Just as good."

Lance knew he wasn't on solid ground with this conversation, but he asked anyway, "OK, if they price it higher because of their advertising, and it has higher administrative costs, I guess they can justify it? I've never seen Jet gasoline on TV. Is that the reason? Why don't we advertise?"

"Really don't have to, Lance. We operate our refineries lean and mean. Once a customer starts buying our gasoline, he stays with us. It's just as good as Chevron's or any of the others."

"But do they put some special chemical in their gasoline to justify their price?" Lance wasn't exactly buying all of JB's explanations as he continued, "There has to be more to a major station's charging a higher price than an unbranded one. The public would demand to know the difference. Performance would make the difference, wouldn't it?"

"No, Lance, we don't know what they put in their gasoline; it just doesn't make it any better, any different. It's sort of like a tube of 'voodoo juice.' Ya hear what I'm sayin'?"

"OK, JB, if you say so. But I do know I've been using Chevron for my Highlander. My dad got me started on it when I got my first car. It seems to work pretty well; I've never tried Bellflower's Jet in my car." Lance regretted that he had been using Chevron's gasoline. That admission wasn't too cool in front of a man who worked for Bellflower and probably had its crude oil in his veins.

"Well, you're going to have to switch. You'll see it doesn't make any difference. Your car will run just fine—no problem, same gas mileage, and you're going to save a lot of money." JB kept a pleasant smile on his face as he continued talking, not mentioning that Lance would get free gasoline in his company car.

"I will. That's the least I can do while I'm working here at Bellflower. Thanks for your time, JB; I really enjoyed talking to you. I'm looking forward to talking to your other process managers and your health-and-safety manager. I'm learning a whole lot about refineries. It's been fascinating."

As Lance left his office, JB laughed quietly at what he had told the young man. He hadn't used the term "additive" but had instead used a new phrase: "voodoo juice," one he had thought of at the moment. He could have used the usual term "mouse milk," but he didn't. Thinking about their conversation, he figured that Lance would believe whatever he told him, because the young neophyte was completely out of his element; he had lots to learn.

CHAPTER TEN

Lance was beginning to have a better idea about how this refinery operated. He knew he had much more to learn, but he now felt his next task was to become better acquainted with the town's mayor and the director of the Chamber of Commerce.

When he had previously talked to the chamber's Linda Livingston, she gave the distinct impression that the refinery was the pride of the town, loved by the neighbors, and was a good corporate citizen. Lance felt that surely there must be some negative issues that were not being revealed. Hopefully, he would get both sides of the story in subsequent objective discussions with the leaders of these two organizations.

Lance felt that talking to the mayor would be helpful in getting the real story of refinery operations and its effect on the town and its neighborhoods. Monica called to set up the appointment, and true to her earlier statement that she knew where most of the bodies were in the town, she gave a comprehensive summary of the actions, views, and politics of the mayor and his council.

"Mayor Larry Sims has been the mayor here for the past six terms. The council follows him like a bunch of lapdogs. There are rarely any disagreements or conflicts between them. They are conservative, anti-union, but for the most part, they leave the refinery alone, only occasionally calling here to complain about odors, noise from flaring, things like that. They do listen to their constituents, but generally speaking, the neighbors have been relatively comfortable with us here, seldom causing any kind of an uproar. But there are those times when they do squall and bawl, and that's when the mayor calls us. Larry talks a lot but is generally regarded as a good mayor in this town. By the way, his re-election is coming up soon. This time, however, he will be challenged by one of the town's liberal activists. The word on the street is he's going to have a battle on his hands."

"Thanks, Monica. That was very helpful. There's nothing like knowing some background on the person you're about to meet. I look forward to meeting him next Monday at ten o'clock. I have a map. I can find City Hall."

Lance had a quiet weekend; he even started reading about refinery operations from the book JB gave him. It was written in layman's terms, and having heard from JB, it was beginning to be more understandable. He and Flash connected at Lance's apartment, but in somewhat of a truce, both agreed not to discuss refineries, particularly Bellflower. Flash took him to a popular restaurant on the beach, the Sandpiper, and introduced him to prawns and chardonnay, neither of which Lance had ever had; he liked both and was beginning to be comfortable in Long Beach.

Lance arrived promptly for his Monday-morning appointment with Mayor Sims. The mayor greeted him warmly, asked him about his background, and welcomed him to Bellflower. "Lance, we're very pleased to have you here. I hope you enjoy this town; they're very nice people."

"Thank you, Mayor. So far, I've been spending most of my time getting acquainted with the refinery and its operations. I've never been in a refinery, but the staff there has been most helpful, and I'm beginning to get the hang of it, although there's still a lot to learn.

"My job is to be your direct information source—to you, the council, and the neighbors—as to what's going on at the refinery; conduct tours; visit the nonprofit organizations; and explain how and why a refinery operates. It's that simple. In that regard, Mayor, are there any issues you have about the refinery that cause or have caused any unrest with our neighbors?" Lance wanted to get that question out front rather that receive a cluster of platitudes about how great the refinery was, the good jobs, and so on.

"For the most part, you guys over there are operating pretty well; however, as of late, there's a lot more noise coming from your flares, and the petroleum odor has increased considerably over the past few months. The neighborhood around you is led by a young firebrand, fellow by the name of Roy Douglas, who keeps calling me and some of the council about those noises and smells. Lately, he has called about the train noise, the switching of cars around at four in the morning, which has become a nuisance. He tells us that the refinery doesn't respond to his complaints, has a deaf ear. That's not good, Lance. You might wanna meet him and talk to him. Ya see, the refinery has a lot of good jobs; it's a great place to work, good pay, good benefits, but saying all this, nobody wants to live next to a nuisance. Right?"

"You're so right, Mayor. I'll go meet Mr. Douglas right away and try to make amends for us not dealing with his complaints. Lemme talk to Pete and his superintendent about those complaints and see what can be done to deal with 'em. Nobody needs to live next to a nuisance. Nobody."

The mayor's report certainly conflicted with the previous positive words of the chamber's representative. One would think that she was living on a different planet. What was actually going on there? Not responding to the neighbor's complaints about increasing noises and odors was unacceptable. He'd deal with that immediately—that would have to change.

Lance thanked the mayor for his candor and promised to talk to the refinery manager and do whatever he could to start more active and responsive communications with the neighbors. He was confident that Pete would listen to him and agree to start improving communications with the neighbors. That was his job. That was his immediate challenge.

CHAPTER ELEVEN

Thinking about what his approach to his refinery manager would be, Lance first decided to learn a little bit about flaring, odors, and train operations. At least knowing about these would give him some idea as to what the problems were and how to deal with them. The trains' operations and schedules were easy to review. How to change it might be a different matter.

He asked Monica to recommend someone for him to discuss these issues with. Whatever additional information he could get would make it easier when he met with the refinery manager.

"Charley Jones would probably be the best one. He's our health, safety, and environmental manager; he deals with all of those issues and should be able to give you some straight answers. I'll call him and set you up to meet him." Monica was more than proving her worth to Lance. She was well acquainted with the negative issues and community animosity regarding refinery operations. Lately, she hadn't received any direct calls from the neighbors. If there were any complaints, they weren't being addressed by anyone in the refinery. That much was clear to Lance. They appeared to be going to someone in operations. As to who and when, she had no idea.

"Thank you, Monica. Since you really haven't had a public-relations person on board here in the past few months, I can understand the breakdown in communications, but that's why I'm here. I can begin to fix that, starting with Charley Jones. He should have some insight on ways to improve our community relations."

Charley was unimpressive when Lance first met him. Thin, with wire-rimmed glasses and a small frame, he looked more like a college professor and in fact resembled Lance's history teacher. However, after a short time in conversation, that initial image changed dramatically. The man had it all together. He knew refinery operations, was pleased to talk about them, and clearly had his finger on the pulse of the community.

"First, let's talk about flaring, Lance. It's about when the plant equipment becomes overpressured. A pressure relief valve is used that automatically releases gases and sometimes liquids through a stack. These tall stacks have pilot lights so that the system is always ready to safely combust the gas and liquids. Your predecessor once said facetiously, 'It makes for a great navigational aid for ships at sea.'"

"OK, but how noisy is the flaring in the neighborhood?"

"Flares can be noisy every now and then, but the neighbors have to understand that flaring is necessary. It's a critical safety procedure, and the process and system here represent the most advanced technological equipment available. Without relieving the pressure, bad things happen—explosions, fire, release of toxic emissions, and so on."

"How about toxic emissions coming from the flaring? Are there any?"

"Flaring can be a contributor to toxic emissions like methane and other sulfur compounds, which are known to cause respiratory problems. Yes, that can happen if the flares are improperly operated or there's a breakdown on the air-pollution devices. We monitor that very carefully here, and the Air Quality Management District (AQMD) keeps a close watch on it. The agencies report that no toxic emissions are being circulated to the neighborhoods, which is good news. However, the neighbors complain that the flaring is causing all kinds of such problems and is a nuisance."

"Charley, I believe I can go to the neighbors to explain flaring and relieve some of their anxieties. Has that ever been done?"

"Not that I know of, but it should be. And you're going to try that?"

"Definitely. That's going to be my first priority. Now, how about that train noise?"

"Yeah, that has been and continues to be a problem. We've talked to the railroad, and they explain that deliveries to and from the refinery are difficult to plan. Ya see, we don't have such a friendly relationship with those guys. Never have, but you may want to go over there and talk to them."

"Yes, but no neighborhood should have to endure such noise at three or four o'clock in the morning. That's a nuisance, and I don't think they want the AQMD to come down and throw the book at them. As a suggestion, why don't you and I go over to the local rail office and see if together we can develop a better schedule for deliveries? That shouldn't be too much of an issue, but I would think they would want to discuss it, not ignore it."

"I've tried, but they don't seem to want to listen. We can try again. Let me set it up. It should be an awakening on your part, attempting to negotiate with the railroad. Their schedule seems to be locked in, and I can't quite figure out why. I'll work on getting a meeting set up for us as soon as possible. They just don't seem to get it."

CHAPTER TWELVE

Now that he knew a little bit about flaring and early-morning train traffic in the nearby neighborhood, Lance felt much more confident visiting with Pete to discuss some of the present concerns of the neighborhood. He had no idea how the plant manager would react to what Lance told him. There would never be a better time than the present. The only way to implement an effective PR program was to have the plant manager become an integral part of the process.

Monica made the appointment for the first part of the following week. Pete was at corporate headquarters in Denver and wouldn't be available until then. During the interim, Lance continued meeting some of the other process managers, being briefed about their special responsibilities. At each briefing, he came away impressed with their knowledge and their commitment to safe operations for employees and contract workers on-site. They all expressed concerns about the community understanding the refinery's obligation to safety and the process issues at the plant.

To his surprise, they wanted to know more about him, what he would be doing at the refinery, and his plan to communicate with the neighbors, the chamber, the city council, and the media. None had any respect for his predecessor indicating that the man was continually aloof, completely ignorant of operations, and appeared as if he couldn't care less about the refinery and community relations.

As he met with the various managers, he was buoyed by their interest and nodding heads. Lance outlined his public-relations strategy and plans to use every means available to communicate honestly and candidly with all. Expanding further, he planned for more tours, presentations to the chamber and service clubs, a possible community advisory council, open house at the refinery, and more involvement and financial support for the various nonprofits in the community. Lance asked for their support, and they enthusiastically agreed. Now, he hoped that Pete and his senior staff would be equally supportive. Time would tell.

Monday morning found Lance waiting for Pete to arrive in his office. Scheduled for eight o'clock, Pete didn't show until almost nine. With no excuses for his delay, he arrived, barked at his secretary, Lora Elliot, for coffee, glanced momentarily at some the correspondence lingering on his desk, and welcomed his guest. "Well, good morning, Lance, how's it going?"

Lance replied in a clear and enthusiastic voice, "Doing quite well, Pete; I'm really enjoying being here. Got settled in my apartment and met last week with most of the managers. Really good meetings!"

"Well, that's good. What's on your mind?"

Lance reviewed his visits with Superintendent DeWitt and Health and Safety Manager Charley Jones, and before he could mention meeting the mayor, Pete interrupted and said, "That's good. You need to know what they do around here. I'm very pleased with their work. Damn, JB has been here longer than I have. He's the best. Who else?"

"I also visited Mayor Sims, and he…"

"Yeah, I know that ole degenerate. He's been around here for a long time. He doesn't give us any trouble, nor does that stupid city council. Their brains aren't exactly in full supply over there, but they pretty well go along with what the mayor tells 'em."

"Have you ever had them over here for a tour?"

"Oh, hell no. There would be no use for that. Hell's fire, they wouldn't even know what they were looking at anyway. I just keep 'em at bay, let them run the city and me this refinery. And by the way, I feel the same way about the neighbors. Oh, yes, they complain now and then, try to call me, but Lora won't let 'em talk to me."

"Pete, if you would, please have the calls Lora takes from the neighbors transferred to me. What are they complaining about?"

"Oh, the usual things, flaring noises, odors, stuff like that. I just don't pay any attention. As I told you when I met you, I'm here to run this place, to make money for the company. I don't need them or anybody else to tell me how to do my job. Understand? Now, back to the mayor, was there anything on his mind?"

Lance took a deep breath, knowing what he would report would either set the man off or have him totally discount what was said. "Pete, he wasn't exactly being negative, but he did say that one of the neighbors, a fellow named Roy Douglas, had called him recently complaining about the refinery's odors, the noise from the flare, and the train noise in the early morning."

Pete shrugged off those complaints and replied, "Well, isn't that too bad? Yeah, I know all about the guy. Bull gave me the scoop on him. Douglas is kind of the rabble-rouser in the neighborhood. He's called here, but I haven't talked to him. Really don't intend to. What did you tell the mayor?"

"I told him that I would go visit this guy and see if I couldn't talk to him, try to explain…"

"Wait a minute, Lance. No way are you going to talk to this nut. Just let him stew. We don't need to explain nothin' to him. You've got better things to do. Understand?"

At this point, Lance had to take a stand. Either he was going to represent the refinery as its spokesperson, or he would just roll over and do what the refinery manager wanted him to do. He took the former stance and forcibly said, "I understand what you're saying, Pete, but I really can't represent the refinery here by not trying to communicate with our neighbors, the mayor and council, or even the media. I've been briefed about flaring here, odors, and even the train noise, so I'm confident that I can at least tell our story and attempt to provide some logic about what we do here.

"If you don't want me to do that, then lemme make it perfectly clear. I took this job as your public-relations guy, and I thought it was completely understood that I would be the spokesman at the refinery. Now, you've changed the rules. If you don't need me in this role, I can leave right now!" Lance had never imagined that he would be able to talk to this seasoned, experienced manager in that way, but he had, and now he waited for the man's response. It was Armageddon time in Bellflower.

Pete's face turned crimson and twisted as if he were being faced with a verdict of guilty. He paused and responded, "Well, well, well, just listen to you. Who do you think you are? My boss? I have to say, I like your spunk. No one has ever talked to me like that. No one around here. OK, I understand what you're saying. You're right. You weren't hired to be a lackey for us. You were hired to represent us, but lemme tell you, you can talk to the neighbors, the mayor, even that nut Roy

Douglas, but don't ever forget that you must tell our story based on facts, not a response to their emotions and unfounded complaints.

"I'll back you up, but we're not going to change a damned thing around here as far as our operations are concerned. We can justify everything we do here, and if it's necessary to make adjustments, we'll look at it as long as it doesn't interfere with our making money. I just don't wanna be forced into something as a result of demands from the neighbors and the council for us to change how we operate. Now, that's your challenge, so work it out, and show me what you plan to do to get the neighbors and council off our backs."

"Fair enough, Pete, but again, have Lora transfer those calls to me; I can handle that. Here's what I plan to do immediately. Briefly, I want to do the following: First, start tours for the council, the chamber, and the neighbors, and advise them that I'm the man they need to call if they have issues; then follow up and meet with them, speaking honestly and candidly. Second, set up an advisory council made up of neighborhood leaders to meet with me and some of our managers about refinery issues that are affecting them adversely. Third, brief the media on refinery operations. And lastly, become more involved with some of the nonprofits in town and the area. I suggest that our refinery managers and some of our operators join their organization and provide financial support. That's about it, Pete. Agree?"

"OK, Lance, I'll agree, but again, let me tell you, we do not bend to their demands. No way. We'll listen, of course, but our responses will be based on the facts and how this refinery is run, not on emotion. One thing, though, as far as the media is concerned, I've been beaten around the ears in the past for our lack of response to a refinery incident, like a fire or chemical release. That's not gonna change. I just don't want to talk to the lame-brain media. They try to screw us up at every chance. I don't like 'em at all."

Lance continued his aggressive position on the issue. "Pete, if you agree on an open dialogue with the neighbors and council, then we must take that same position with the media. Their problem is they don't always understand what and why we do things around here, therefore, when we have upsets, if they've been briefed beforehand, they'll have some understanding of what happened and why. For sure, we don't ever want to lie to them, but we don't have to tell them everything either. When we don't get our story out fast and accurately, believe me, there are other sources they can contact that will give them the real story.

"In that regard, we can start doing media training for our managers, and we can develop a crisis-management plan so that when an upset occurs, when we are fined, whatever, we will be able to implement the plan and deal with it effectively and efficiently."

Coming out of his chair like a rocket launched, Pete charged over to Lance's chair and yelled, "Now, there you go again. I don't ever want any of my managers being taught on how to face the media in an interview. That's your job. Neither me nor my managers will ever go on TV or radio. That's you, your job, my man. That's you! Understand?"

"I hear you, Pete, but without training, if I'm on vacation or over in Denver, and something happens, who's gonna represent the refinery? Monica? That role has to be taken by someone who has been trained. He or she may never have that responsibility, but it could happen."

Pete quickly snapped, "OK, but in that case, we'd have someone from Denver be our mouthpiece. They'd have to do it, not my men."

"No, Pete, the media will want to have someone from our refinery to tell them what's going on. That's the way they operate. The media training I do would, at least, have an experienced and media-trained refinery manager. It's not that complex or difficult. Once we have the plan, it's simple—just follow it."

"OK, but let me look at the plan before you start training. I must approve it. Again, Lance, I just don't agree with your approach to the neighborhood, council, or the media. I just don't have any confidence that we'll be able to change their minds on what we do here. I really don't, but for now, I'll go along with it. If bad things happen, then all I can say is, 'I told you so.'"

"Fair enough, Pete. What I'm proposing is not rocket science. It's common sense."

"Yes, but, you sound like an experienced PR guy. Hell, you were a reporter. How did you get so smart? What experience do you have?"

"Well, just trust me. As a reporter, I had to act the same way—get the facts, tell the truth, don't make it up or try to avoid it. Communicate and report it honestly. Like I just said, it ain't rocket science. Just trust me, Pete; we're going to be all right."

Now broadly smiling, Pete said, "OK, PR man, now get the hell out of my office. I've got work to do. Git!"

"I'm going, Pete, but as Schwarzenegger has said, 'I'll be baaack.'"

Lance felt like he had just climbed Mt. Everest. He was exhausted, but he believed he had turned the corner and felt strongly that public relations at the refinery were on the right track. Progress had been made, but he knew there was still a long way to go.

He now had to connect with the neighborhood firebrand, Roy Douglas. He'd check with Monica to see if she knew the man; maybe she lived in the immediate neighborhood. He'd get on that early next week. Right now, he needed to call Flash and see if they could get together. It had been a long day. He was more than ready for a little R and R.

CHAPTER THIRTEEN

Flash was more than ready to meet Lance for a drink or two and dinner at the Pacific Wave. He certainly didn't want a repeat of their last experience there.

Driving his company car, Lance picked up Flash, who immediately started his usual tirade about working at a refinery, taking all those perks, and trying to tell the public that it was really a safe place to work and own a house at its fence.

"Come on, Flash, enough of that. Hey, I'm pretty happy over there. They've really been good to me. I'm learning a lot about the equipment there, what it does and so on. So, give me a break. No more about it. Deal?"

"OK, old friend, 'deal.' But I still can't believe you're working at a refinery. You need to be at a newspaper. That's what you went to Chico for, to learn to become a journalist, a reporter. Now, you're a flack for a refinery? But, I promise; I won't talk about it anymore, at least tonight."

Friday night at the Wave was at its roaring best. Band playing, dancing, drinking, and lots of good-looking women gathered together at tables, looking for someone to buy them a drink. It definitely was *the* place to be on a Friday night.

Lance and Flash sat down at a table next to two ladies, who met their eyes quickly. A blonde and a brunette, both "hot" and seemingly ready for action.

Flash made the first move, leaned over to them, and said, "Hi, I'm Flash, and this is my friend, Lance. Can we buy you two gorgeous women a drink?" Both smiled, and the brunette, the shorter of the two, leaned forward to better show her well-endowed breasts, helped by a sexy, low-cut cocktail dress. She replied, "Flash? I bet you could really run fast."

That caught his attention, and he replied, "Funny you'd say that. I was a track man at Chico State. A sprinter."

The ladies looked at each other in an "as if we really cared" way and immediately took Flash up on his offer. "We'd really love a drink. Chardonnay would work."

Flash motioned to the waitress and ordered the wine. He and Lance each ordered a beer. On a roll, he introduced Lance to the ladies and said over the continuous noise of the band and the crowd's frenetic conversation, "Now, you know who we are; what are your names?"

The blonde spoke first, saying in a low, husky voice, "I'm Lana." Indeed, there was a lot of Lana there at the table—a striking beauty; engaging, dark eyes; with her hair flowing softly down her back. She didn't stand up, but she didn't need to. There was no question who the major player was in that group.

"I'm Cindy; I'm Lana's mother," the brunette laughed, attempting to further lighten up the conversation. "I'm always her chaperone when she comes here. I have to keep her safe from you lecherous men." Cindy's perky personality impressed Lance; he felt that there just might be something there in his future. Tall, with green eyes that radiated her face well, this lady was definitely a "showstopper."

They all laughed heartily at this tongue-in-cheek introduction. "OK, Cindy, who's *your* chaperone?" Lance asked. Another round of laughter erupted, which followed with Lana saying, "Cindy doesn't need a chaperone; she's a black belt, tough as nails, and no man in his right mind would even think of messing with her. Hey, what about you two guys? What about you?"

Lance, now feeling quite comfortable with this conversation, boldly said, "Well, actually, we're both priests, so why don't you come over with us so we can protect you?" This was an opening line, and he amazed himself; he couldn't believe he had said that.

Lana jumped at their offer and said, "All right, 'Father,' but I know you won't be staying with us for long. Church will be calling soon?"

Flash responded quickly, "No, ladies, not tonight. It's the four of us; no church 'til Sunday. By the way, what do you two ladies do for a living? Who's first? Take it, Lana."

"I'm a dental hygienist; I do 'mouth to mouth.' And looking at your mouths, believe I could do wonders for you, ya think?" Her mischievous smile more than aroused both of the men.

"I just bet you could, Lana; I just bet you could. Cindy, what about you?"

"I'm a stringer for the *Long Beach Press Telegram.*"

Lance quickly jumped on that comment and said, "Interesting, I'm the public-relations man for the Bellflower Refinery. I bet you could string along with that, couldn't you, Cindy?"

"A PR man for a refinery? That sounds like a smelly job. One thing about *there*, you can always know when you're *there*, can't you? The place always smells like an oil well."

Lance winced at that remark and countered, "Yes, but we're working on that."

"I just bet you are. Planning on closing it down and getting out of town?"

More laughter, and then Flash picked up the conversation. "I'm no oil man; I'm in the marketing group with Hughes. It's a really good job, no smell at all, and I'm very happy there."

"Marketing?" Cindy asked. "What do ya do?"

"Right now, we're working on an updated plan to make the Internet more attractive for people to buy our product. Ever heard of Hughes Net?"

"No, I haven't, Flash," Lana responded. "That sounds like a better net for the trapeze guys at the circus."

The four continued bantering back and forth throughout the evening. The wine and beer flowed continuously; the repartee between them was lively and often irreverent. Cindy asked in a smiling voice, "OK, you two brothers of the cloth, don't you think it's about time you started preparing your flock for confession?"

"Oh, you are impossible, Cindy. But I really like your and Lana's style. Uhh, where do we go from here?"

Lance didn't like Flash's aggressive question. They had just met these two ladies. Was he suggesting that *we*? He simply wasn't comfortable with that approach.

Not missing a beat, Lana answered, "Don't know about you, but I'm going home. I have a seven-o'clock patient. I need my rest."

Cindy added, "I'm going home, too; I'm doing a story about a lady who started a company making tortillas. She is using her mother's recipe that has been in the family for years. Business has been brisk; it's the talk of Long Beach about how good they are. I'm meeting her at her shop early in the morning. Hopefully, she'll have a few samples for me."

"OK, you two gorgeous ladies, at least we can walk you to your car and say good night. It has been a real blast being with you this evening. Did you come together?"

"No, silly, we came in separate cars. Who wants to walk me to mine?" Lana asked, peering directly at Flash.

"Yeah, I'll have the honor of walking you there," Flash said proudly, "but, Cindy, beware of Lance. He just might want to…"

Lance grunted and said, "Fear not, Cindy; I will need to start confession in the morning. I'm going straight home, too."

Opening the VW Passat's door, Lance said quietly, "Cindy, it was really great meeting you and Lana. I'd like the pleasure of calling you. I don't wanna be so pushy, but may I have your phone number? I'd like to call you soon. We could have coffee and get better acquainted and…"

"Certainly, I'd be happy to. But please don't take me to the refinery; I don't need a tour over there." She wrote her cell-phone number on the back of her business card and handed it to Lance.

"No worry there. I promise. I'll call you soon, and good night." He held her tightly. She felt so good, and he gave her a light kiss on her cheek. He was smitten with this stringer; he wanted to see more of her.

As Cindy drove home, she called Lana on her cell. "Hey, Lana, this guy, Lance, asked me for my phone number. He wants to take me out. I think he's kinda cute."

Lana answered, "Great, Cindy, but this guy, Flash, wasn't so lucky. He asked me out, too, but since Rolf and I are seeing each other, I didn't think I needed another man in my life at this time."

"Well, Lance does seem interesting; I just might take him home and housebreak him, but I've got to know him a lot better." She laughed to herself and thought, *Housebreak? Now, that just might get a little kinky.*

They had their first date shortly afterward. They agreed to meet for coffee at Starbucks. Lance enjoyed it immensely. The conversation was light, nothing serious. He really was turned on to her and wanted to see her again. Cindy also appeared interested. Her good humor continued as she filled their two hours with one-liners that had Lance enjoying every minute of it; he had never had such an experience. He definitely wanted this relationship to prosper.

CHAPTER FOURTEEN

O n Monday morning Monica retrieved Roy Douglas's phone number, and Lance placed a call. There was no answer; he left a voice-mail message. Hopefully, Douglas would call him. He'd wait and see.

About five o'clock that afternoon, Douglas called Lance, who was still in his office. "Hello there, this is Lance."

With no hesitation, Douglas started the conversation in a gravelly voice, "I don't know you, sir, but I appreciate your calling me. You're the first guy from the refinery who has ever called me. So, whadda ya want?"

"Thank you, Mr. Douglas. I'm Lance Wilson; I appreciate your calling me back. I'm the public-relations man here at Bellflower. If we could, I'd like the opportunity of getting together. I understand you're upset about our operations here, and I'd like to talk to you about that."

"Look, Mr. Wilson, I've been complainin' about your damned re-finery, the odors, the toxic emissions from the flare, and the overall nuisance you guys are to our neighborhood. Yes, I'd like to meet with you tomorrow. I'm the assistant manager at the Safeway store; I get off around four thirty. How about we meet at Denny's, say around five?"

"I would like that, Mr. Douglas. What time?"

"See ya about five." The phone line went dead. Clearly, Roy Douglas wasn't one for trivia.

Lance couldn't believe a chance to meet this neighbor would come so soon. He'd be ready for him, confident that he could at least try to deal with the usual complaints. He didn't tell Pete about the meeting; he didn't need to hear any more of his negative feelings about complaining neighbors. Lance would, however, report the meeting's details later—that is, *if* it was productive.

Lance arrived promptly at five o'clock, and there was his contact sitting in one of the booths just off the entry foyer. He was well groomed, dressed appropriately as an assistant manager, and good looking, although there was a scowl on the man's face, which was hardly welcoming.

Lance took a deep breath and shook hands. Getting right to the point of their meeting, Douglas started, "Look, Mr. Wilson…"

"Hold it, please call me Lance. If I could, may I call you Roy? I don't think meeting like this means that we need to be so formal. Agree?"

"Of course, Lance. That'll work. As you know, I'm a neighbor across from your southern fence line; I've lived here about ten years, have a wife, two kids, both in elementary school. As I told you, you're the first guy from the refinery who's even had the courtesy to talk to me. Much less meet with me. I was really surprised to get your call."

"Well, Roy, that's changing as of right now. Go on. I'll listen to what you have to say. Then we can talk about what you think should be done."

Douglas briefly went through all of his complaints—the odors, the flare's noise, and its spreading toxic fumes in the neighborhood, causing all kinds of breathing problems. "Yes, we call the Air District; they investigate but continue to tell us they've talked to you and confirm there are no emissions from the flare that are causing any concerns. We just don't believe 'em. We believe you and the district are in cahoots with each other, both protecting each other."

Responding to that charge, Lance strongly said, "No, Roy, that's simply not true. We have air-monitoring devices all over the plant. The Air District monitors the air 24-7.Believe me, if we were polluting the air with toxic chemicals, we'd be told, and if we didn't correct it, they'd close us down. Simple as that."

"Yeah, I hear ya, but we just don't believe you or the Air District. I've done some research and found out that you guys could put scrubbers in those units, which could be used to remove some gases like carbon dioxide from your refinery exhausts. What about that?"

Lance couldn't wait to respond to that charge and said, "Yes, we have scrubbers, and yes, they clean the air of the various pollutants. By the way, I plan to organize tours at the refinery, invite the neighbors, and let them listen to our process managers, who can explain how we operate. What do you think of that idea?"

"Yeah, that's probably a good idea, but I don't think the neighbors are going to believe a word you say. They're just fed up with the way you guys operate. Some residents even talk about having a demonstration there at the gate. They are just fed up."

"All right, but I believe we can explain the scrubbers in a reasonable, truthful way that the neighbors will understand. What other issues do you have?"

"Oh, yes, another issue is asbestos. I have neighbors who live on the northern fence line, and they see you guys are demolishing an office building, all wearing masks. Why masks? Because you're removing asbestos—your workers are wearing masks to protect themselves from the ill effects of asbestos, a known carcinogen that after exposure can cause cancer. In that regard, one of my neighbors has just been diagnosed with mesothelioma, and any workers or neighbors who have worked in and around asbestos are all threatened with that disease."

"Yes, I'm aware of that, but…"

Roy interrupted Lance and roared, "*Your* workers are wearing masks, but you haven't issued one word of warning to the residents living near the fence line. Nothing. Whadda ya say to that?"

Lance was blindsided with that news. He paused, shook his head, and said, "I was not aware of that. We'll correct that immediately. That is unacceptable."

"And that's just the point, Lance. You guys don't have any communications with the neighbors; it's as if you don't want to tell them what's going on. It's as if you really don't give a damn. How do you explain that?"

"I hear you, Roy. I really hear you. I can assure you, I can promise you that will change. We'll make ourselves visible to your neighborhood—tours, citizen advisory councils, one which I'm sure you'll want to be a member of. That's my job, and I intend to put those plans into action right now."

"Oh, come on, Lance. Do you really think that refinery manager of yours, that guy who's been around for at least ten years, is gonna approve all that? You gotta be smoking funny cigarettes. He's just not gonna do it."

"Roy, yes he will. I've talked to him, and he's on board. Communications with the neighbors will be vastly improved; you can count on it."

"Talk's cheap, Lance. I'm originally from Missouri; that's the 'show me' state. You'll have to show me. The ball's in your court."

The meeting came to an end. Both had made their points. Now, Lance's words had to be turned into action. Lance would schedule an appointment with his boss immediately. Hopefully, their recent conversation had begun to sink in, and the road would be clear to complete the plan and implement it.

CHAPTER FIFTEEN

L eaving the meeting, Lance called Lora, Pete's secretary, left a message, and requested a meeting with the man as soon as possible. It was important.

He received an answer early the next morning; the refinery manager could meet him at 11:00 a.m. Lance wished it could have been sooner, but he'd take what he could get. As he came into Lora's office, she asked him what the meeting was all about.

Lance answered quickly, "It's about the dismantling of the former offices on the north side of the refinery—workers there are wearing masks, removing asbestos, and not informing the neighbors."

"Oh, that's terrible. He won't like to hear that. I didn't know that was going on, and I wonder if he did." At least she understood the problem.

As Lance entered the boss's office, Pete was already standing up behind his desk. He said, "Lance, it's lunchtime; let's go over to the club, and we can talk there. OK? I need a drink."

Lance had never been invited to lunch with Pete. It was at the Long Beach Country Club; he didn't even know where that was located. "That'll be fine, Pete. I've never been there."

There was no comment from Pete as they motored over, through upscale neighborhoods, down a long driveway, and into a southern-plantation-like building that impressed Lance mightily. Andre LaMarche, the maître d' greeted Pete warmly and said, "Welcome, Mr. Peterson, nice to see you again. The usual for you, sir?"

"Please, Andre, the usual, dry martini on the rocks. Andre, let me introduce you to our new public-relations director at the refinery, Lance Wilson."

"Nice meeting you, Mr. Wilson. May I get you a drink?"

"Thank you, Andre. I'll have a Bud Lite."

"Certainly, sir, coming right up."

Andre led his guests to their table in a most militant manner. The view was breathtaking at the first fairway as it sloped gently down toward the first hole. Tall pines sheltered the verdant, well-groomed grass. Lance had never been to such an elegant and high-class country club; he was duly impressed.

Lance had no idea that his boss would be drinking martinis at lunch. Certainly, his former editor, Ralph Wiggen, would never do that; he didn't even know that his former editor drank.

"Well, Lance, what's on your mind? Lora said you had to meet with me soonest. Do we have a problem, or did you just want to have lunch at the club?"

"No, Pete, I wanted to give you an update on my meeting with Roy Douglas. He…"

Pete exploded and yelled, "You met with that guy? I wish you hadn't done that. Why didn't you tell me? I would have put the stop to that right then."

"But, Pete, I told you I was going to do that. I just felt that talking to him, getting to know him, and hearing his complaints would give me an opportunity to hear him out and try to explain refinery operations to him."

"That's BS, Lance—that guy is not going to listen to you or believe anything you tell him."

"I don't agree, Pete. We had a good meeting. I believe I made some progress. When I told him we were going to start tours at the refinery and set up a community advisory council, he seemed to like the idea."

Taking a long sip from his martini, Pete answered, "And you think he liked the idea. Hell's fire, he just can't wait to call us and the mayor again and start that same ole song and dance we've heard so many times."

"Have faith, Pete; I think I am making progress. And by the way, he did tell me one thing of which I was totally unaware. He said that we were dismantling one of our old office buildings on the north side, removing asbestos, and our workers were wearing masks to protect themselves."

"What's the matter with that? Of course, they should be wearing masks. I wasn't aware that it was going on. What's the deal?"

"The deal, Pete, is that the neighbors really didn't know what was going on. There are houses right up to the fence line, and seeing workers wearing masks, they kinda got freaked when they discovered there was asbestos removal going on, and they didn't know about it. They are aware of asbestos's issues. If the neighbors aren't protected, there's a chance of them getting mesothelioma."

"That's ridiculous, Lance; they're not going to get that disease. It just won't happen. We've been dismantling buildings around here for a long time. No one has ever gotten mesothelioma, our people or anyone else." His voice now was reaching a higher pitch; the few patrons there kept looking over at the man and wondering what was troubling him.

"But, don't you see, Pete, the neighbors weren't informed about what was going on. They were in the dark. When we do something like that, so close to where they live, we must either communicate with them with letters or have meetings here at the refinery. That's the right thing to do."

"I'm sorry, Lance. I just don't agree. Those neighbors aren't stupid. They know how to protect themselves without our telling them what to do. I just don't agree."

"I hear you, Pete, but at the very least, I want our health-and-safety man to write a letter about the dismantling to relieve any fears they might have about mesothelioma and possibly suggest that masks, if they feel they're needed, would be available at the refinery. It wouldn't cost much and would be a good-faith gesture on our part."

"OK. But I just don't think it's necessary. It's a tempest in a teapot. Have Charley Jones draft a letter, let me look and approve it, and then I'll sign it. Is that what you want?"

"Yes, it is. It's the right thing to do."

"I'd like to have another martini, but that'll have to wait 'til the cocktail hour. We'll eat and get back."

Charley drafted the letter; it was clear and concise and gave the neighbors a summary of what was going on at the fence line. Lance liked the tone and gave his approval, and Pete, after a little bit of editing, signed it. The letter went out to all the fence-line neighbors.

In the next few days, Lance received a call from Roy Douglas; he thought the letter was excellent, and he thanked Lance for making it happen. A similar call came to Pete from, of all people, the mayor. Pete still didn't quite understand the positive response. He still felt it was unnecessary to communicate with the neighbors, notwithstanding what his PR man had suggested. He had a refinery to run, not a feel-good PR program. In his view, there was definitely no revenue or profit in making people feel better. After all, his job was production, and good production produced the smell of money.

CHAPTER SIXTEEN

Lance had Cindy's cell-phone number; he decided to call her and make a date. He was a bit nervous; it had been quite a while since he'd done that. But after meeting her and so enjoying the hip repartee between them, he made the call.

It was late in the afternoon. The phone rang three times, and a sleepy voice whispered into the phone with a barely audible "Hello."

Yes, Lance was sure that was Cindy's number, and upon hearing her voice he said, "Hey, Cindy, this is Lance Wilson. How are ya?"

"Who?" she sleepily asked.

"Lance Wilson. Remember me? We met at the Wave last week. I'm the PR guy from Bellflower."

"Oh, Lance, of course; I'm so sorry. I just had not woken up when you called. What's up?"

"I'm thinking that you and I need to get together for dinner soon. Would that work for maybe tomorrow night? I know that's rushing it, but I really would like to see you again."

After a lingering pause, Cindy answered, "Yeah, that'll work. Where do you suggest we go? Any ideas?"

"No, you decide. I'm new here and don't know many places. We'll go where you decide."

"All right, Lance, let's try one of my favorite places, Amarillo Al's. They make the best fish tacos I've ever had, and their margaritas are to die for. Sound good?"

"Great, I love fish tacos." He had never even had one. "What time? Shall I pick you up? You'll really enjoy my Vespa scooter. OK?"

Before answering, she thought, *A Vespa scooter? He has to be kidding. What do I say to that?*

Noting her pause, he quickly added, "No, Cindy, I'm only kidding. I'm driving a Ford Fusion, four doors and all. Where do you live?"

"I live at 5890 Sand Dollar Lane. It's a rental, number 2B, on the second floor. How about picking me up at six? I'll be wearing high heels; a long, flowing dress; and a new, wide-brimmed picture hat. I'll try not to be overdressed, but it is a very fancy place; only the beautiful people go there. We'll fit in fine as long as you don't say you work for Bellflower."

Her shrill laughter raced through the phone. He loved her humor. They were going to get along just fine.

"Fine, see ya at six. I was going to be dressed as Darth Vader. Do ya think that'll be all right?" Both laughed as if they had known each other for years.

Later, Lance went to MapQuest, found the correct directions, and headed to Sand Dollar Lane, a neighborhood known for a series of apartments rented by young professionals. He bounded up the stairs and rang her bell, and as she opened the door, he just stood there and gaped at her. He was at a loss for words seeing this fashionably dressed lady, a brunette with glistening hair, dark-green eyes that laser-beamed right through him, form-fitting slacks, and a blouse that nicely brought out her fantastic body.

He reached for her hand, but she pushed it away, came closely to him, wrapped her arms around his waist, and kissed him deliciously, her hot tongue swirling around in his mouth, back and forth, up and down. She softly said. "Nice to see you again, Lance. Welcome to my little house. Shall we get comfortable?"

Lance was completely blown away with Cindy's loving greeting. He knew he had no experience with a passionate woman. His steady at Chico, a churchgoing Baptist, had never made such a move. His tight jeans shielded his passion to a degree; his body shielded nothing. He was on fire. Yes, on fire, a twenty-three-year-old virgin who had never had any experience quite like this. He liked it; he wanted more.

"Would you like a drink, Lance? I have most anything you'd like." He wanted nothing to drink; all he wanted was standing there right in front of him. "No, I don't think so. Could we just sit down here on the couch and talk?"

"Oh, Lance, we can talk later. Why don't we just go to my bedroom and, well, get better acquainted?" Lance couldn't believe what was happening—he barely knew this lady; they had met less than two weeks earlier. It was first at a bar then coffee. There was no kissing, no talking dirty, no messing around, and yet, this lady came on him like a longtime lover.

His lovemaking was amateurish. He frankly didn't know what to do. She knew everything and was completely, totally uninhibited. He had been living in a cocoon; he was sexually "out to lunch."

His orgasm came quickly, after virtually no foreplay. All he wanted to do was rest on the bed with her, talk softly, and enjoy the experience. She wanted none of that; she wanted more sex; she was insatiable. He tried again, but the experience left him virtually with "no 'tane in the tank."

Wanting to say something, he mumbled, "Cindy, do you want to go to dinner now? I bet you're hungry. Yes?"

"Oh, I guess. Lemme freshen up, and we'll go over to Al's." Retiring to her bathroom, she frankly was disappointed with her new friend's sexual inexperience. She knew it must be his "first time." He was simply inadequate; he did absolutely nothing for her. Thinking more about him, she mused, *I really like this guy; he's quite handsome, but I need to housebreak him, bring him into the twenty-first century. Maybe I can get him to read* Fifty Shades of Grey, *and he can practice what he learned. That'll be a tutorial for him. Maybe then he'll come around. If that won't work, nothing will.*

There was no more sex that evening. They ate heartily and talked until Al's closed. Both talked about their past and their schooling. She went to a private Catholic girl's school, majored in journalism, worked in a paper in her hometown of Hemet, became bored, was a hostess at a Long Beach restaurant, met a reporter for the *Long Beach Telegram*, lived with him briefly after he got a job for her as a stringer, and left him high and dry but continued with the paper. Her feature writing became popular, and she was content to remain unmarried, with no interest in being anything else. She frankly admitted she was a party girl and just wanted to have fun; she could get serious later. There was lots of time.

Hearing Lance's background, she just couldn't believe he was a PR man for a refinery. "Lance, Lance, Lance, what in the hell are you doing? What were you thinking? You? You're so much better than that. Get out of that job; go back to doing what you were trained to do. Go back to reporting hard news at a newspaper. Do it now before they suck you into the corporate world and you can't or won't want to get out. You'll make too much money; you'll become a slave to the corporate mentality."

"All right, Cindy, I hear you; it's the same thing my friend, Flash, tells me, but in all seriousness, I'm beginning to enjoy my job. I'm finding that the refinery's management, for some reason, has a reluctance to communicate with the city, particularly with their neighbors who live right on their fence line. I believe I can change that and bring Bellflower into the real world. Sure, the manager there is a neocon, a hard-line manager. When I first met him and complained about the odor outside the fence, ya know what he said? 'Son, that's the smell of money.' Can you believe that? It's true, and he really believes it... totally. Ya think I don't have a challenge there?"

"Yes, Lance, you certainly do, but it's one I wouldn't touch with a ten-foot pole. Good luck, my man, good luck. Let's call it an evening. Let's do it again real soon. I really like you. I think we can make some beautiful music together. OK?"

"You bet, Cindy. I completely agree. I'll call you soon."

Driving back to his apartment, Lance couldn't believe the evening he had had. He knew he had fumbled his effort badly to make love to Cindy, but he'd do better next time. Yes, he knew he had to do better, because she just wasn't going to stand for some amateur, some man of his age with the lovemaking finesse of a sixteen-year-old. Sex obviously was her game, but down deep, she had much more to offer than that. He was sure of that. He wanted to get to know the "real" Cindy.

CHAPTER SEVENTEEN

With the apparent success of alerting the neighborhood about the asbestos-removal project, Lance thought it was now time to implement a tour program for the neighborhood. He still was a bit ignorant about all the refinery's units, so he spent the better part of two weeks visiting and revisiting the process managers. With that completed, he felt relatively comfortable conducting a tour.

He notified the neighborhood activist, Roy Douglas, and suggested that if he would give him a list of names, he would call them personally and invite them for a tour. Roy agreed, and after a few days of inviting people, Lance had a list of about thirty names, addresses, and phone numbers. With support from Monica, he made the calls for the tour to start Saturday morning at 9:00 a.m. All, with few exceptions, agreed to come. Those who declined were adamantly hostile, saying such a tour was purely a public-relations trick; they wanted no part of it.

The group met in the refinery's lobby and retired to the conference room. Coffee and sticky buns were served, introductions made, hard hats furnished, and a general presentation held about refinery operations—how the crude was manufactured into gasoline, diesel fuel, and so on. It appeared to hold the neighbors' attention.

Lance then took them on a walking tour, viewing each of the processing units. He stopped briefly when one of the neighbors asked, "What is that tall unit in the distance?" Lance hesitated a few seconds, realizing that he didn't quite know the answer, and replied, "Why, that a BRT."

"A BRT? What's that?" yelled one of the neighbors.

Lance laughed and said, "Why, that's a 'big round thing.'" All clapped and laughed energetically, and another said, "Oh, I get it, if that's a BRT, then that one over there is an LRT." Again all laughed, and together they yelled, "Little round thing." With that, the tour group bonded. They became courteous and attentive and asked lots of good questions. Units like the catalytic reformer unit, hydrotreater, and distillation unit became familiar as to how they related to the operations. Explaining these units' functions at a *"Reader's Digest level"* made the difference. Lance felt really good about what had happened; he believed that future tours would be equally successful.

Upon leaving, high fives abounded between neighbors and Lance. He felt like a rock star who had just performed in front of five thousand screaming fans. He couldn't wait to report to Monica, and even without an appointment, he stuck his head in Pete's office and delivered the good news.

Pete had no one else in his office; he waved Lance inside and wanted to hear more. "OK, my boy, so your tour was successful, but we just don't have the time to keep doing this. The next thing you'll want to do is have some of my managers conducting the tours; they simply don't have the time to do that. That isn't what they're being paid to do. So, if you want to have tours, then you're going to be the one to do them. Understand?"

"Pete, I don't agree. The tour today was only about an hour. Surely your managers could spare an hour to do this. We could get, say, five to ten managers; I would brief them on the format and give them the experience of talking to neighbors about what goes on in a refinery. It's just good business to do that; it pays off big time."

"Nope, I'm just not gonna approve that. As I said, that's your job, Lance, so if you want to continue giving tours, you're the one who's going to be doing it."

Lance didn't like or appreciate Pete's attitude or decision. He'd live with it, but he believed that when the neighbors' letters started arriving and applauding the tour, that would change Pete, and he would insist that all managers get on board as tour guides. At least, he thought that it might turn out that way.

Sure enough, the letters started arriving. There were no criticisms from anyone; they hoped that the tours would continue. One letter stated, "I've lived next to this refinery for ten years, and I had no idea what was going on inside except noise, grinding, big trucks, and smelly odors. Thanks to the tour, I now have a much better understanding. Bravo to Mr. Wilson and the refinery."

Lance was now on a roll; he was gaining momentum with his plan. The only obstacle he could foresee was the continuing negative attitude of his boss about an aggressive public-relations and community-outreach program. That would change; he was confident of it, and he continued his training outline for the managers. His goal was to have them involved in the tours.

CHAPTER EIGHTEEN

That weekend, he and Cindy got together again. This time, his lovemaking improved considerably with some "this is what I like" talk from her. She explained how the book *Fifty Shades of Grey* had made her much more passionate, much more erotic, and more uninhibited. He was a more than apt pupil, and the "teacher-student" relationship worked very well.

Their rendezvousing continued throughout the summer, going to the beach and making love in the sand, after which Cindy would say laughingly, "Gee, Lance, we can't keep doing this here. Sand gets into everything."

A few weeks later, as they were driving back from San Diego, Cindy finally asked him a surprising question. "Lance, have you ever smoked marijuana?"

"Good gracious, no, Cindy, I never have and probably never will. I hear that when you start, it only leads to heavier drugs like cocaine, heroin, and so on. I don't need that in my life. I get more than enough high just being with you. I don't need marijuana."

"I figured you hadn't, but would you try it with me, just once? Please?"

"OK, but just for you. Just once."

Driving along at about fifty-five miles per hour, she reached in her purse, pulled out a bag filled with marijuana, removed a paper, and, driving straight ahead, proceeded to roll a joint, expertly and efficiently. Lance sat there with his mouth open, saying nothing. Finally, he spoke, "Wow, I can't believe what I just saw. You rolled that cigarette exactly like my grandfather used to do. Exactly. How in the world did you learn how to do that? It was amazing."

"Well, Lance, the answer is simple—practice, practice, and more practice. Now we have a joint; let's begin to smoke it."

"No, Cindy, not here in the car. We're almost at your place. Let's do it there; I'll be much more comfortable."

"Oh, all right, sissy, we will, but I have to speed up. Time's a-wasting." Her foot pressed hard on the accelerator as the car roared up to almost seventy.

"Please, Cindy, slow down. I want to get there in one piece, not as a cadaver. Please!"

"I hear ya. We should be there in a few minutes. Hang on."

Arriving at her apartment, they both galloped up the stairs and in a total frenzy began to disrobe, scattering clothes in all directions. Cindy reached back in her purse to recover her jewel of a joint, picked up a book of matches, and said, "Now, Lance, since you've never tried it…"

He interrupted her lesson and said, "Cindy, I've never even smoked a cigarette. Never. As an athlete, smoking was totally prohibited by our coaches, and had we ever been caught, that would have had us kicked off the team. It just wasn't worth it to even try. OK. Now tell me what to do."

Like an automechanic instructor telling his pupil how to tune an engine, Cindy began the tutorial and lit the joint. "One thing you must not do is, for the first time, inhale deeply. If you do, you'll start coughing heavily. So, easy does it."

"Inhale? How do you inhale?"

"Here, watch me." She took a drag off the joint. "Now, take a deep but a light, inward breath, hold it momentarily, and then blow out the smoke."

The odor from the marijuana was nothing he had ever smelled before. He thought that smelling the smoke was what got a person "high."

"OK, Cindy, I get it now. Smell the smoke and you get high. Right?"

"Oh, Lance, you are so wrong. You get high by inhaling, holding it, and then blowing it out of your mouth. So, try it now, and do exactly as I showed you. Take it slow and easy."

"All right, here goes." Lance performed the procedure exactly like his instructor had showed him. But he hadn't quite listened to his instructor; he inhaled entirely too deeply and immediately started to cough.

Cindy laughed at her pupil and said, "Oh, my, Daddy's got the cough. You didn't listen when I said to inhale lightly. Now, try it my way."

Like a student who had been corrected by his teacher, Lance performed the second time, precisely as he had been taught. "Ya know, Cindy, I don't feel a thing. When is this going to hit me?"

"Sit down, my love; sit down here on the couch; relax and let it happen. You're gonna feel it real soon, and you're gonna feel real good."

In about three minutes, its effect began to sweep over the student, an effect of pure relaxation, resulting in conversations that he had never thought of having, setting him free as he babbled somewhat uncontrollably and found out what many of his friends had experienced. He began to laugh hysterically, noting that he now knew how stupid it was for Bill Clinton to say, "I tried it, but I didn't inhale." Did anybody really believe such a statement?

Cindy looked at her pupil, enjoying how his smoking had changed him. He had a new personality, laughing and making totally off-the-wall statements that made absolutely no sense. When asked about it later, he didn't remember.

As this continued, Cindy went to the refrigerator and pulled out a half-eaten package of Mrs. Field's chocolate-chip cookies. Lance had previously enjoyed them; now he devoured them, gobbling down about a half dozen. "Whoa, Cindy, I've got the terminal munchies. I can't get enough of those cookies. Take 'em away."

"They *are* away, all gone."

"Let's go out and get some more. I need more." One would have thought he hadn't eaten in a week.

"No, darling, no more; I now have plans for you. Come with me to my boudoir, my love."

Making love stoned was an exhilarating experience for Lance, so much more enjoyable than his first time with Cindy. He felt he had been doing this all his life. Thank goodness for Cindy and her marijuana. He was totally relaxed, and his mind was a fountain.

Later, Lance began to talk about the success he was having with the first tour, the candid conversation he had with the neighborhood activist, and the fact that he now better understood the issues the refinery faced with their operations.

"Ya know, Cindy, there's a lot more I could do there, but the refinery manager is a Neanderthal in the modern world. He just doesn't get it. He objects to everything I offer him to do in the area of public relations and community outreach. I believe he's slowly coming around, but not nearly as fast as he should. I need him to get with the program."

"How does he feel about dealing with the media? For example, what if the refinery had a big fire or maybe a heavy release of toxic fumes that swept over the neighborhood? Would you guys be prepared for that?"

"Good question. I posed the idea of developing a crisis-management plan, doing media training with him and his managers. He really wanted no part of that. He let me know that dealing with the media was *my* job, not his and his staff. Under no circumstances would they be involved with the media."

"That's ridiculous, Lance. What if the 'sand hit the fan' there while you were out of town, on vacation, going to a conference, visiting Denver's headquarters? In other words, you wouldn't be there to deal with the media and, of course, the neighborhood."

"Pete just blew that off, saying, 'We're never going to have an upset like that. Never have. We run a safe operation here. It's just not going to happen.'"

"Never? Bad things do happen to refineries. Look at what happened up in Benicia just last year, a big oil spill in the San Francisco Bay, killing ducks, coating commercial fishermen's and private boats with crude oil. A disaster, but those guys handled it very well. They were out front telling the stakeholders and the media what happened and how they were dealing with it. Can you imagine if something like that happened here, and you weren't going to talk to the media or the neighbors? Give me a break."

Cindy paused and added, "Lance, I'm never going to tell you how to run your job, but lemme suggest something I learned long ago as a reporter. When you're suggesting something and the management refuses to go with it, put it in a file, write a memorandum, whatever, but keep written notes in the event you're ever challenged for something you proposed and it wasn't implemented. I guess it's called a 'cover your ass' file. I know I keep one, and I'd suggest you do, too."

"That's a good idea, Cindy. In this case, I haven't, but I will, starting right now. As a reporter, that was exactly what I would do, but for some reason, I haven't been doin' that here. If Peterson doesn't go along with me for a plan I've suggested, like media training for managers, I should have something to show that protects me. It's proof I tried."

Cindy laughed at the thought she had given a PR man a suggestion and said, "Well, my dear, I gotta mark this day down as monumental. I gave an idea to a PR man, and damned if he didn't take it. Now, here's another idea I'm having. I'm going to do a story about your refinery's community-outreach program, the tours and so forth. It'll be a positive piece and should help its image. Needless to say, oil refineries don't get much good press, you know?"

"I like that, and I could be the spokesperson for the refinery. I'd have to get the old man's approval, but I think I can. Lemme get back to you on that."

"I have an appointment with the Big Brothers Big Sisters' head person to do a feature on their organization. The work they do with their matches—an adult paired up with a boy or a girl from a family where divorce or separation has taken place—it has been incredible. Oh, by the way, Lance, wanna take a joint with you and use it the next time you talk to your boss?"

"Please, Cindy, I wouldn't want to take the chance…however…"

CHAPTER NINETEEN

Pete had to approve the idea for Cindy to do a feature story on the refinery's outreach program. Lance was confident that he would go for it, but knowing the man, he'd want the writer to let him review and approve the copy. That was strictly a taboo; most writers would never consent to that.

When Lance arrived in midafternoon, Pete was still in his office, upset with the news that his financial man had accepted a very lucrative offer from Osco Chemical; it was just too good for him to pass up. Pete couldn't meet the offer, so he wished him well and got the "help-wanted" request off to Denver headquarters.

As usual, Lance had no appointment with Pete, but he wanted to get Cindy's proposal to Pete for his approval as soon as possible. He stuck his head in the doorway and quickly described Cindy's idea.

Pete broke in on Lance's explanation and asked, "A question, Lance. Do you know this reporter? Have you ever met him?"

"It's a *she*, Pete. I've met her and seen some of her work. She's good, writes well, and we'll get a good story. Trust me."

"OK, but if she shows it to you, you approve it, and then she changes it, you're going to be in trouble. I don't trust the media. You just can't be too careful."

"Gotcha, Pete; I'll handle it." No, he wasn't exactly honest with his boss. Yes, he did know the reporter, in more ways than Pete would ever know. However, their relationship had nothing to do with her reporting skills.

He left a message with Cindy, gave her the good news, and asked that she call him and make an appointment for her to come to the refinery and do the story. Cindy got back to him promptly; she'd come over at his convenience. The following Tuesday was scheduled,(;?) her first visit to Bellflower.

Lance had done his homework for the interview. He also called Roy Douglas, told him what was happening, and asked if it was agreeable to meet with her. He accepted graciously; although he had never been interviewed by the media, he was comfortable with doing it.

Monica met Cindy at the central office door, escorted her to Lance's office, and asked, "Have you ever been to our refinery, Cindy?"

"As a matter of fact, I haven't. I pass by it on the 405 on my way to appointments, but I have never had the opportunity to visit. I look forward to meeting with your public-relations man. I've never met him, either. Has he been here long?" Her façade was notable. She thought laughingly, *I might change careers.*

Their meeting in his office was pleasant and relaxing. Monica commented later to her boss, "There was certain chemistry between you two; one would have thought you guys had known each other for a long time."

After the interview, which, to no one's surprise, went well, Cindy left the refinery and connected with Douglas. That interview also went well; he did bring up the refinery's past lack of outreach, but he praised its improvement. He didn't exactly say "it was love in the cottage," but there was no question that he felt the refinery had made great progress with community outreach in the past six months. Overall, Roy was becoming a proponent.

Lance reviewed the draft and had some doubts about Douglas's negative comments covering the refinery's indifference to the neighborhood, but, in his view, that was the really good point about the refinery's outreach program. The article stated that outreach had been poor but was now much improved. He hoped that Pete would understand that, too.

When the feature was printed in the paper the following week, Pete read it, went ballistic, called Lance into his office, and read him the riot act. "I should have read that piece of crap before the *Telegram* published it. You did and for some reason thought it was all right, but it stinks. Why did she bring up the past and our obvious disinterest in being a good neighbor here? She didn't have to print that. She should have focused on what we're doing now."

Lance listened patiently, letting the boss blow off his steam, and finally responded, "Pete, have you talked to any of your managers about the article? Had you done that, you would have heard very positive comments. I've talked to many of them, and they were very pleased with what was written about us here. You must understand, Pete, from what I've heard from the neighbors, particularly Roy Douglas and many on the recent tour, their attitude about us has changed significantly. They think we are finally getting our act together. And certainly the article confirmed that. I just think you're wrong about the article; in my view, it was very positive."

"You said that you talked to some of our managers, and they liked it. I hadn't talked to any of them, but I'm surprised, really surprised. I guess I was looking at it the wrong way. I might have been wrong. I'm sorry I sounded off like that. I apologize for jumping off too soon. I just thought…"

Hearing Pete give an apology was a rare thing. In six months at the refinery, Lance had never heard one from him. "Thank you, boss, I really appreciate that. And by the way, I still want to draft a crisis-management plan and do media training for the managers and even you and JB."

"Lance, I want you to forget that. You're the guy who'll be dealing with the media, the guy who'll be interviewing them. That's your job. We don't need a plan to do that. The only plan we need is the plan to deal with some refinery upset, investigate what happened, and make sure we don't do it again. Is that clear? What we need here is a corrective action plan to document what we do to clean up any mess we have here."

"But what if I'm not here? What if I'm climbing Mt. Whitney and out of cell-phone range? Who's gonna hold the media's hand then? Please, let's not face that situation; let's be prepared. Please!"

"Lance, one last time. Don't ever bring this up again. Do you understand?"

Lance nodded, turned around, and left the room, shaking his head. He had not been able to break through Pete's reluctance to even think about such a plan. Hopefully, there would never be a major upset that would result in local and national news. Over the past five years, there had not been one serious incident at the plant. He hoped that it would continue. He didn't even want to contemplate such a thing, but it could happen. The possibilities were endless: fatalities, significant environmental damage, major evacuations of the neighborhood, substantial property damage, major media coverage, and the negative public and government perception that Bellflower's operation just might have to be closed down.

His company car needed an oil change. His earlier meeting with Bull, the refinery's maintenance manager, had not gone well. He knew he would have to avoid him, especially since he and Pete were longtime friends and drinking partners.

Lance made the appointment to have his car serviced. He would leave his car there while he walked back to his office, only a few blocks away. As he got out of his car at the garage, Bull met him. Something was obviously wrong; there was no smile, only a deep grimace on the man's face.

"Mornin', Bull, how's it goin'?"

"Not good at all, my boy, not good at all. I'm really disgusted with the way your public-relations program is going around here. Tours, lots of people here in the refinery and then this god-awful article that appeared in the paper. Where in the hell is this lady coming from? If you read the article, you would think that we're a bunch of bad actors around here, not caring anything about the neighbors, or for that matter, anyone else. I happen to think that this refinery is a good place to work—safe, good pay, good benefits—but that wasn't mentioned. All it mentioned was how bad it used to be. I thought the article was just BS, and I told Pete what I thought. And ya know something, he agreed with me. He was really upset."

"Yeah, I know. I talked to him, tried to explain that, in my view, it was a good piece. I told him that I had heard good comments from some of the managers, and he seemed to cool down; he hadn't heard that, and…"

"Well, for Chrissakes, I sure as hell wasn't one of 'em. I thought it was really bad. Lemme tell you, Lance, I don't like what you're doing here. We were doing just fine 'til you came, and now you're adding all of the silly stuff trying to make us look good. We don't need you here. I wish you were leaving tomorrow."

Shocked by his comments, Lance answered, "I regret that, Bull. I'm only doing what I think needs to be done to get the neighbors and the city council to understand and appreciate that we are a good neighbor, and..."

"Yada yada yada, Mr. PR Man. Save that stuff for someone else. I don't need to hear it. Your car should be ready in an hour or so. I'll have one of my men drive it back to your office; the keys will be in it."

"Got it, Bull, and thank you for servicing the car." Lance was completely taken aback by his ranting and raving. Maybe he didn't understand what he was supposed to do around here. For sure, he didn't think he'd spend any time with the guy to explain it. He wanted to avoid Bull at all costs.

CHAPTER TWENTY

Despite the unsettling confrontation with the maintenance manager, Lance was pleased with the early success of his community-outreach plan. There would be more tours, hopefully with some of the process managers involved. He'd also start firming up relationships with the city council and the chamber's executive manager. First things first: communication with the neighborhoods was his priority.

He received a most positive response from both the council and the chamber. Both applauded the refinery's tour program, acknowledging at the same time that community outreach there had not been much of a priority in the past. He was invited to the chamber's annual meeting and the council to present his plan. All were greatly appreciative; all gave their full support.

The issue most critical to him, however, was the lack of a crisis-management plan and especially media training for the refinery's manager and his staff. In that regard, Pete had made his position very clear: "No, hell no, and don't bring it up again!" That position made the refinery vulnerable, particularly if there was an incident and he was not available on the scene to talk to the media and the neighborhood.

That issue was put on hold, as the weekend was about to start. He had not seen Cindy since the past weekend; he missed her madly, her lovemaking, and, especially, their smoking marijuana. Aside from those pleasures, he was beginning to really care for the lady. He had never had a relationship like hers, a far cry from his Chico steady. Their conversations revealed a person with depth, one who loved life, but not so much that her long-term journalistic interests would not be realized and achieved. He couldn't wait to see her again.

His concerns with refinery management occupied much of the early conversations they had as they met for breakfast. He was very open to her. However, Cindy continued to criticize his wasting his time, shortchanging journalistic talent for a job as an oil refinery's PR man.

"Yeah, Cindy, you're right. I can't get newspaper reporting out of my head. I miss it so. I took the refinery job as a temporary pass-through, knowing in the future I'd probably go back to newspapers. It hasn't happened. Frankly, I'm rather enjoying being at Bellflower, vastly improving their image, strengthening relations with the city, the chamber, and the neighborhood. The big problem I have is dealing with the refinery manager; he's old school, focusing entirely on bringing an excellent return on the company's investment and enhancing the company's stock and so on. He says it's the smell of money."

"OK, I hear ya, Lance, but let's forget this for a while; I have plans for you. Let's go to my place; my loins are humming for you."

Whatever was on Lance's mind, his concerns soon evaporated as the marijuana and uninhibited sex occupied him completely. He had not read *Fifty Shades of Grey*, but her goal that morning was to teach her dedicated student one movement at a time. She did so expertly, and he was an apt pupil.

They relaxed for the rest of the afternoon, listening to Dave Brubeck, one of the truly best ever to play jazz. Another round of smoking right about six o'clock that evening was interrupted by the beeping sound of Lance's iPhone. Bellflower was calling.

Thinking out loud, he mumbled, "Hmmm, I wonder what they want?" He answered, "Hello, this is Lance."

"Lance, this is Dick Reynolds; I have the duty here this evening. I hate to bother you, but there's a fire in the health-and-safety building. Can you get down here as soon as possible? The fire department is here, and Channel 7 just called; they're on their way."

"Got it, Dick; I'm on my way. Should be there in about twenty minutes if the traffic is not bad. It is rush hour, you know. I'll do my best." He knew that after spending the last eight hours at Cindy's place, sipping a little wine and smoking dope, he really wasn't in any kind of shape to face the media, or for that matter, anyone else down there. He was loaded.

He yelled to Cindy, telling her what was happening, and she asked, "Do ya want me to go down and…?

"No, please, stay here. If the newspaper wants you to cover it, they'll call, but I imagine they'll get one of their beat reporters to go. I doubt whether they would need you."

"How bad is it? Would any of the gasoline tanks down there be in trouble?"

"Doubt it, 'cause the building is on the other side of that area. Gotta go, love. Later."

With the heavy southbound traffic, his speed, for the most part, was at a crawl. This gave him a little time to clear his head and focus on the situation; his confidence increased, but he knew he wouldn't be at his best. "Damn," he mused. "I hope I don't screw up and make a fool of myself."

Arriving at the refinery, he could see flames bellowing out from the building. Firefighters were on the scene, their hoses spouting huge streams of water at the source. It didn't look too serious, but it surely would make TV's ten-o'clock news. To his relief, by the time he arrived, his dope-and-wine-filled head had cleared; he was totally confident that he would be at his best to deal with the incident.

As he went through the gate, Superintendent DeWitt rushed over and said, "Hey, Lance, glad you're here."

"Yeah, I would have been here a lot sooner, but the freeway traffic was horrible. Has the media arrived?"

"Yeah, they called, but they're not here yet. I guess they got caught in the same traffic you did."

"Well, they'll want to talk to us. Can you or Dick give me some facts about the fire so I can talk to them?"

"You're gonna want to talk to them? Are you kidding? You don't have to tell 'em a damned thing. They'll only screw it up, tell a story that is much, much worse than it is, and the neighbors, the town'll freak out. Lance, this fire'll be out very soon. It'll be over before they'll even be here."

Lance nodded and responded, "JB, of course I will talk to Channel 7 or any other the media that arrive, TV, radio, or print. That's why I'm here. That's what I do."

"But, Lance, I don't think the old man would like that. He's been burned by those bastards in the past; he doesn't trust them."

"Let me deal with Pete. Now, just give me the facts. When it was discovered? Why the fire? Any injuries? Any threat to any of the gasoline tanks there? How much property damage? And so on. For those questions, the media likes damage estimates. I'll tell 'em 'that will be investigated.' We'll give no estimates of damages at this time, only when we'll have a better idea.

"After I've talked to them, I will put together a holding statement and send it out to those who were here, the other media, and city hall. Actually, this is not a big deal, but they have to know that we're available to speak to the media in the event any future incidents happen here."

"All right, Lance, but you'd better talk to Pete when he gets back. He went deep-sea fishing this afternoon, and he'll wanna know what you did."

"JB, I can handle the boss. Trust me, and thanks for being here, and especially thank Dick Reynolds for getting the crew on the scene and dealing with the fire. It was good work."

Channel 7 and radio station KGN arrived and requested a refinery person to talk to them. Lance stepped up, accommodated them for pictures, and interviewed at the scene. He had never met any of the media before, but he now knew that in the future, he would need to do that to develop relationships. That was the way the game was played—he knew he should have done it earlier.

With the fire now completely out, Lance made his way back to Cindy. He called her on the way, reported positively about the incident, and suggested they go out to get a bite to eat. He was famished, and chocolate-chip cookies weren't quite going to help him much, but later, he was sure they would.

Lance regretted being stoned when the call for help came. Needless to say, that was totally unprofessional. Would he quit smoking? No, refinery upsets were not a daily happening, but in this case, his smoking could certainly make him vulnerable. He was lucky, but he did recover very well. Perhaps a stress situation had a positive effect by alleviating the high. He didn't know, but he wasn't going to spend a lot of time investigating it.

Lance called Lora to set up an early Monday-morning appointment to visit with Pete and brief him on the fire incident. Pete was essentially pleased with the report, but he again reminded Lance that there was no need to have a crisis-management plan, noting that the refinery knew what to do, procedures were in place, and they had him to deal with the media and the neighborhood.

"Thank you, Pete, for your support. However—and I know you don't want me to bring it up—but we do need to have some media training, have something on paper as to who to call, how to create an effective holding statement detailing what happened and what the refinery is doing about it."

"Lance, damn it, that's your job. You're the guy who'll do all that. Now, one more and the absolute last time, don't bring it up again."

CHAPTER TWENTY-ONE

Lance was feeling pretty heady about his initial experience with the media. True, the setback was hardly earthshaking, but he thought he had handled it well. He had dealt efficiently with the media and gotten a holding statement out later that evening and then a follow-up with the *Press Telegram's* editors and Channels 7's and 10's news editors. All went well; he was beginning to be at home with his position, although in this business, as the story goes, there's always something.

While he was now the guy making the news, he still missed being the reporter who covered the news. He just couldn't get that out of his system, but for now, he'd stay with the refinery. There was still a lot of work to do. He wanted to see it through to the end.

Late one Monday afternoon, about a week later, he received a call from his new friend, Roy Douglas, the community activist; he seemed upset, agitated, and speaking in a loud voice, he yelled, "Lance, this is Roy. You and that goddamned refinery you work for have got to do something about the odors here. I swear they're getting worse. You told me you were dealing with it, some cock-and-bull malarkey about scrubbers, how they corrected the smell. But it just ain't working."

"I don't understand, Roy; I haven't noticed any here lately, but…"

"Well, this past weekend, I don't know what went on over there, but the place stunk up worse than ever."

Before Lance answered, he realized he hadn't been down there the previous weekend; he and Cindy had gone over to Palm Desert for a tennis tournament at Indian Wells. Nobody had called him from the refinery about any odor issue. "Roy, I wasn't aware; I was out of town. Lemme check on it, and I'll call you back."

"OK. I'll wait to hear from you. I thought you had that stuff under control. I thought the odors had really been a lot better lately. No, they're back, and we are really pissed. Nobody needs to live next to a nuisance, and you bastards are a nuisance." Roy's demeanor had definitely reverted back to a full-time community activist. He hung up with an emphatic click.

Lance called his superintendent and asked if anything unusual had happened last weekend that caused an unusual case of foul odors. JB reported that yes, there was an upset, a malfunction at one of the air-pollution units, but it was corrected right away.

"JB, I wish you had called me; we could have gotten out a letter of explanation and apology to our neighbors. What I heard this afternoon was that it was really bad."

"Oh, well, Lance, they're always complaining about something, odors, noise, whatever. After all, they're not living next to a cemetery. There's bound to be some noises and odors now and then, but that's the way it is with a refinery. Tell the complainers to lighten up; he should be glad we're here. We pay good wages and make Bellflower's economy a lot better."

"JB, I know how you feel, but can we get one of the process managers to give me a call and provide me easy-to-understand material to explain what happened? I'll draft a letter for Pete's signature, and we'll get the letter out by tomorrow."

"Boy, are you getting defensive in your job. You mean, every time we have an odor incident here, you want to send out a letter to the neighborhood, apologize, and ask their blessings? As far as I'm concerned, that's simply going too far. We don't need to do that. I'm sorry, Lance, but I just don't believe it's necessary."

Lance had heard that stuff before; he had heard it from Pete, now the superintendent, and even the maintenance manager, the guy who took care of his car. "I hear you, JB, but our relations with our neighbors, whether you agree or not, are very important to this re-finery. I don't think you would want to live next to a nuisance—a noisy manufacturing plant, a bar full of drunks. I know I don't, and you don't either. So, let's do the best we can to respect our neighbors and operate here as safely and quietly as we can."

"OK, Lance, I'll have Tom give you a call about the upset, and then you can write the damned letter." With that, the line went dead. JB was just one more refinery employee who still had an unsupportive attitude toward the importance of proactive community outreach. It was no longer the nineteenth century. Times had changed. JB, like Pete, needed to get on the bandwagon and support his PR program.

CHAPTER TWENTY-TWO

Lance was slowly falling in love with Cindy. No, it wasn't the drugs or the sex that was influencing him; it was the bare fact that he thoroughly enjoyed her company. She had depth, soul, and a keen interest in reading and writing. He felt that she should be able to do much more with her journalism talent, but at that point in her life, she was content to be a stringer for a major newspaper.

From her side, she continued to press him to make a change back to journalism, remove himself from those at the refinery who had no interest in public relations. They were interested only in operating professionally and efficiently. Public relations had no place in their respective lives and operations; that was Lance's job.

He sat at his deck, pulled his documentation file, and inserted his working notes with the community letter. Then it hit him! There appeared to have been no follow-up from the railroad and its schedule to deliver products out of the refinery. He knew the neighbors on the north side of the fence continued to insist on a change. They were at a loss as to why there hadn't been any effort to deal with the issue. Charley Jones had met with the railroad management earlier, discussed the issue, and received somewhat of a limp declaration that they would look into it. Nothing had changed, at least not yet. That had to change.

He called Charley to enlist his help again and to meet with the railroad about the early-morning delivery times. "OK, Charlie, let's go back over to see those thugs, read the riot act to them, tell 'em the neighbors are about to go to the Air District and demand they cease and desist from those practices. You do know that if the neighborhood goes to the local paper, that should put some pressure on them. However, knowing how the railroad operates, they'll put the blame squarely on the refinery. Whatever, let's get on it right now. You set up the appointment, and we'll double-team 'em."

"Will do, Lance, but I've dealt with them before. Big windup, no pitch. Promises, but no action."

"Well, this time we won't be nice guys. They'll completely understand we're damn serious."

After his telephone conversation with Charley, he began to think how aggressive he had become with senior refinery managers and operators. If these guys hadn't known he was no patsy, they certainly knew it now. He had never shown that kind of temperament in his life. Maybe it was Cindy's influence. Whatever, he intended to ratchet it up even more. He had nothing to lose.

He and Charley met two days later with the railroad's manager who was responsible for train deliveries out of the refinery. Eric Leming was a twenty-five-year veteran and a person that reflected "no nonsense" in his dealings. He had never been involved in early discussions, only one of his subordinates. Having him there perhaps signaled that the railroad was ready to talk.

He wasted no time in stating the railroad's position. "All right, gentlemen, my foreman told me about your previous meeting over here complaining about the noise. Let me make our position here very clear. We have a delivery schedule to meet, and you guys can't tell us when we'll make it. So, there. Whadda ya have to say about that?"

Charley took the lead and replied, "Now, Eric, let me make *our* position very clear. We're the customer, and we'll work with you to develop a delivery schedule that does not create a noise nuisance with the neighbors. That shouldn't be too difficult for us to work out. In other words, if we didn't have the product for you to deliver, then there'd be no reason for you to be involved, but we do, and all we're asking is for you and our operations manager to work out a schedule that is amenable to both parties. It's as simple as that."

"Yes, but we like an early-morning delivery and…"

Lance took over the conversation, pointed his finger directly at the manager, and strongly said, "We *know* what you like, but the neighbors are beating us up thinking it's our fault. So, before they go to the *Press Telegram*, let's avoid that and straighten this situation out, starting right now."

Leming's face turned cherry red. He couldn't believe this PR guy was being so aggressive. He paused and answered, "All right, we'll work this out. Have your guys call our guy, the logistics manager, Phil Dawson, and we'll try to change the schedule to accommodate those whiny neighbors. Whatever you do for 'em, they'll never be satisfied."

Charley smiled and added, "We appreciate that, Eric. That's a win-win for everybody—the refinery, you, and the neighbors. Thank you for your consideration." They all shook hands, and both Charley and Lance believed they had finally broken the ice with the man. It had been a good meeting.

Lance and Charley immediately met with Pete and briefed him on the railroad's decision. "Yeah, those are hard-nosed renegades over there. Fortunately, we don't have to deal with 'em too much, but over the years it has become much worse. Thanks, you guys did a good job. Now, we'll see if they do what they say they're going to do. Don't hold your breath; I know 'em well."

CHAPTER TWENTY-THREE

The letter to the neighborhood addressing the refinery's odors seemed to be effective. Roy thanked Lance for handling it, once more repeating his long-held concern. "You guys just never learn. You treat us like stepchildren. First, you tell us nothing, and then when I start yelling at you, you finally come around. When will you ever learn?"

"I hear you, Roy. But you gotta admit, we're doing a lot better, and we're working on improving it. It's a culture thing. In the past, they never had to worry about any kind of community outreach, but in today's world, it has to be an essential part of their operation. Thanks for your comment. I truly appreciate it."

Lance wished his boss had been a "little bird" hearing that exchange between him and Roy. Whether he would have agreed with it, he didn't know, but progress was being made in that area, although in little steps, one at a time.

He hadn't been with Cindy all that week; he missed her. He called and received only her voice mail, which gave him an opportunity to talk dirty to her. After he hung up, she returned his call immediately. "Hey, you smooth talker, I just got your message. I got so excited I was about to give you an advanced lesson on how to give 'good phone.' You were good, but I could make you better. Why don't you come on over? I've had a so-so day; I'm hungry. I need a 'Lancewich.'"

"Give me twenty minutes, and I'll be a-knockin' at your front door."

"That's not good enough. Wish you could fly over."

He really got aroused just talking to this lady. He wondered again how he had gotten so lucky. His friend Flash's relationship with Lana didn't even result in a one-night stand. She and he just didn't click. He said, "No chemistry with the lady. No chemistry." Chemistry certainly wasn't the problem with Cindy and him. None at all.

Walking up the steps to her second-story apartment, his cell phone rang. Hearing it ring now always tensed him up a bit, thinking something was going on at the refinery, possibly an upset or whatever. The last such call had covered the fire at the health-and-safety building, his first experience dealing with the media. That had gone well, but, regardless, he knew such a call was almost certainly not from a friend asking about the score of Chico State's recent victory against St. Mary's track team. "Hello, Lance speaking." There was no caller ID showing who was calling, so he questioned whether this was even a legitimate caller.

"Mr. Wilson, this is Dr. Leon Pullman. I'm the head surgeon at Sacramento Memorial. I hate to call you about this, but your mother and father have been involved in a traffic accident. Both are in the hospital here."

Lance cut in and asked, "Are they seriously hurt?"

"Your mother has a fractured pelvis and a concussion; your father a broken femur. He will be released in a few days, but your mother

may be here for a while. I think she'll be with us for nearly a week or
so."

"Thanks for calling, Doctor; I'll get to Sacramento as soon as I can.
I'm in Long Beach, and driving up there shouldn't take me more than
six or seven hours at the most. Please tell my dad I'm on my way."

The news immediately removed any passion Lance had brought to
Cindy; his parents needed him. "I'm sorry, Cindy; I've got to go. My
parents have been involved in a traffic accident; they're in the hospital, and I need to get to Sacramento right now."

"That's terrible, Lance. Is there anything I can do?"

"No, but thank you, honey. I appreciate that. I'll call the refinery and
let 'em know what's happened, and I should be away for a few days."

She kissed him tenderly and walked him to his car. With tears stream-
ing down her soft face, she said, "I so care for you, Lance. Please be
careful and stay as long as you need, but do hurry back. I'll miss you."

He called Lora at the refinery manager's office and gave her the news.
"I'm so sorry, Lance. I'll tell Pete. Please keep us informed as to your
folks' condition. What hospital are they in? We'll send flowers."

"Sacramento Memorial, Lora. Thank you, I gotta go."

CHAPTER TWENTY-FOUR

Packing hurriedly, he headed his Fusion north on I-405 and then I-5 directly to Sacramento. While he mostly kept the car at the speed limit, seventy-five miles per hour, he would occasionally push it a little harder, cruising at eighty. His thoughts wandered during the drive over his parent's injuries, of course, Cindy—he couldn't get her out of his mind—and finally, the refinery. He laughed out loud, thinking that there might be an upset, and he wouldn't be there to be the mouthpiece. Regrettably, no one else would, either. Pete had made that abundantly clear—that job was his; he would be in Sacramento, a long way from Bellflower.

On the latter issue, he never gave much of a thought. As Pete had said, "No serious upsets in more than five years. We're really safe around here." There was always a chance, but if something happened, it simply happened. His conscience was clear; he had forewarned his boss. Lance had several e-mail documents in his crisis file and phone call notes as well.

Lance arrived about ten in the evening and checked in the hospital to get an update—no change. Both his parents were resting comfortably. He left word that he would be back in the morning and left his cell-phone number in case they needed to reach him. The drive had exhausted him physically and mentally; he was more than ready for bed. The Holiday Inn was only a few blocks from the hospital, making it convenient for him to stay. He checked in with Cindy, reported all was well, said good night, and turned the lights out.

Lance was at the hospital about eight o'clock the next morning. Both parents occupied the same room; his mother was still sleeping, his father sitting up, eating his breakfast. "Hi, Dad, here I am. Just arrived from Long Beach. How ya doin'?"

"Why, Lance. Why are you here? You really didn't have to come. Your mother and I are doing just fine."

The son laughed and responded, "Dad, I'm here because I want to be here. After all, who's going to play gin rummy with you? I bet I can still beat you."

"No. No, you can't. You never have, never will."

"How's Mother doing?

"Oh, she is doing all right. Has a broken pelvis and a concussion. But she's holding her own. The doctor tells me I'm getting out of here tomorrow morning, but she's going to be here for a week or so."

"Are you going to be able to handle it at home with you on crutches?"

"I think so. We have great neighbors, and if I need some help, I'm sure they'll be glad to do so."

"I don't know how long I'm going to be here, but I'll stay as long as I'm needed."

"Well, son, we appreciate that, but you've got a big job down there at that refinery. They'll want you to hurry back home."

"No, Dad. They'll get along very well without me. I've called 'em, and they say I should stay here as long as I need to."

And so, Lance stayed for another four days. His mother was released, and he arranged for a part-time housekeeper and a nurse to look after them. He figured he could start back on Monday morning. His parents agreed, thanked him, and so appreciated his being with them.

Lance was relieved that his parents were now at home and were recovering about as well as could be expected. Both were in their midsixties; neither had any serious health issues. They were going to be all right.

After having breakfast at the hospital, Lance thought he would drive up to Lake Tahoe for the day; he hadn't been up there in several years. His memory of camping there in the woods with his friends, especially after his high-school graduation and all suffering commode-hanging hangovers, came rushing back. It wasn't pretty.

His day was pleasant, and as he drove back to Sacramento, he thought blissfully about his next day's return to Long Beach and, of course, seeing and being with his lady. He was ready to call it a day. Just as he turned out the light, he thought he would catch the late news on Channel 12. What he saw and heard immediately brought him back to reality as the reporter announced that there had been a fire and explosion at the Bellflower refinery—no details of injuries, but the neighborhood had been evacuated due to the acrid smoke and release of toxic fumes. There would be little rest for Lance that evening. He did not relish his immediate future at Bellflower.

CHAPTER TWENTY-FIVE

Lance tried to call JB, but his cell phone was continuously busy. Finally, he answered in a breathless and tense voice, "DeWitt here."

"JB, this is Lance. I just caught the news of the fire on TV. I'm in Sacramento taking care of my parents; they've been in a..."

"Dammit, Lance, why aren't you here? All hell's breaking loose, the fire is still out of control, the fire department is here trying to deal with it, the neighborhood has been evacuated, the media is here clamoring for someone to talk to, and you're in Sacramento. Get your sorry ass down here on the double."

"Where's Pete? I need to talk to him." He knew he'd get nothing but the boss's wrath, knowing that his PR man was not on scene or anywhere in the area.

"Unfortunately, Pete's on vacation visiting his parents in Laredo, Texas. I just talked to him, and he's wonderin' where the hell you are and..."

"JB, he knows I'm in Sacramento—at least, I told Lora where I was going." Lance was becoming more irritated and impatient with every passing minute. "Who's going to talk to the media? The neighbors?

Since there's been an evacuation, they're going to be damned upset. They've been on pins and needles ever since the health-and-safety building fire, bitchin' that we hadn't communicated with them. This thing, much more serious, is going to cause one helluva lot of trouble. How about the mayor and council? Has anybody called them?"

"You just don't understand, Lance; we don't have time to talk to anybody or call anybody. We're goin' gangbusters around here trying to put the fire out, eliminate the toxic fumes spreading over the neighborhood. I'm tellin' you, it's an ugly mess. For god's sake, get your ass down here soonest!"

"I'm leavin' right now, JB, but I won't be able to get there until at least five or six tomorrow morning. I'll do the very best I can." Lance knew it would do no good to remind JB or Pete why it was so important to design a crisis-management plan, not only for when he was there, but more importantly when he *wasn't*. As far as a refinery spokesperson, none had been trained; the most likely person would be Charley Jones, the health, safety, and environmental manager. His knowledge of the potential effects of toxic emissions sweeping the neighborhood would be helpful when talking to the media. He tried to call him, but he knew Charley was tied up and wouldn't be able to talk, particularly to the refinery's PR man. Lance left a message on his cell, telling him he was driving back and to please call him. He wanted to brief Charley before he asked him to talk to the media, but he explained he'd have to get permission from management for that to happen.

Back to talking with JB and then telling him what he planned to do, Lance wondered what the response would be, and he feared the worst. What could happen was for JB to give no such permission. Lance was sure that Pete had already put his foot down about talking to the media. If that order prevailed, the reputation of Bellflower would take a serious hit, one that would take years to correct.

JB answered the call with a voice that was obviously stressed to the max. "Yeah," he yelled, "is this Lance? Where are you? Are you coming down now?"

"I'm about to, but I need your permission for Charley to talk to the media, give 'em a summary of what the refinery is doing to put out the fire and the procedures to stop the toxic emissions. Charley is the best..."

"Hold it, Lance, just hold it right now. I talked to Pete about that, and he said the only person he wanted to be talkin' to the media was *you*. I explained your absence, and it became very clear. No one else."

"But, JB, I'm not there. The media wants to talk to someone there, someone who is on the scene. Oh, sure, I can get the information from Charley, but they want to talk to..."

"I understand, but you're just going to have to do that, talking on the phone as you drive down. I'm sure you can handle it."

Now completely frustrated and angry, Lance knew it was no use to continue to badger JB. He knew that he would follow Pete's order to the end; nothing was going to change. He called Charley, gave him the update, and asked that he give him the details so he could at least sound professional and knowledgeable and respond to the media. Before he got onto I-5, he got out his pad and started jotting down some of the basic facts the media would need to know.

"Lemme have it, Charley, nice and simple."

"OK, Lance, here's the deal. While we're still investigating the exact cause of the fire, what we know is that as operators were stripping away insulation at a leaking pipe, a vapor of flammable substance, similar to diesel, ignited, and the fire broke out. Toxic fumes, high levels of sulfur dioxide, were released, causing the neighborhood to be evacuated. At this time, the fire is almost under control, along with eliminating the release of the toxic emissions."

"Thanks, Charley, a couple more questions. How are the toxic emissions being handled, and when was the neighborhood alerted and ordered to evacuate?" That was the number-one question Lance hesitated to ask.

"Concerning the evacuation, I'm not exactly sure, but probably, I guess, about thirty minutes after the release."

"How were they told?"

"We called the sheriff's department, told 'em what was happening, and they got the word out to the neighbors. I was told that squad cars drove into the neighborhood and broadcast the word."

"Was anybody overcome from the emissions? Was anybody, particularly children, taken to the hospital?"

"Not sure, Lance, but…"

"If they were, we have to take care of their expenses. No doubt about that." Lance assumed such a decision would be automatic—without question, the refinery would assume that liability.

"I can't comment to that, but believe we should and will."

"OK, Charley, that should do it, so if anybody calls, please have the operator transfer those calls over to my cell. I can talk to them as I head south. Knowing the media, I know they'll ask questions I can't answer. I'll just have to tell 'em, 'I'll get back to you on that when

I have the information.' Thanks for all, Charley; I really appreciate that. Please tell JB what you've done. Hopefully, he'll like that; however, at this time, talking to the media is not high on his priority list." Lance laughed at that last remark. He was sure about that.

About fifty miles out of Sacramento, the media started catching up with Lance; they needed more information. Many of the questions he had anticipated; many he really didn't want to answer.

They included:

Does the refinery have an alert system to inform the neighborhood of an incident and recommend they evacuate? If not, why not?

Do you anticipate the Air District and EPA to fine the refinery for its release of toxic emissions?

Any fines over the past five years? How many air violations has the refinery had over the past five years?

Do you think OSHA (Occupational Safety and Health Administration) will levy a stiff fine on the refinery for safety violations that caused the fire? Any fines levied in the past? If so, what for?

Does the refinery have a crisis-management plan? If not, why not?

Did any of the plant get evacuated? Any injuries?

Do you expect the city council and the neighborhood to take any action against the refinery?

All these thoughts swirled through his mind as he drove. He thought of Cindy, wondered if she was aware of the fire at the refinery, and wondered if she would be asked to go there and write a story. Whatever, he called her—he longed to hear her voice, wanting to hear someone who understood what he was going through. Oh, how he wished he were in her bed, making wild, passionate love, high on weed and not giving a damn about anything, just being with her.

It was now near midnight; she would probably be in bed if she had not been called to the refinery. The phone rang three times. Finally, she answered in a sleepy voice, wishing she hadn't answered the phone. "Hello?" She then noted that it was from Lance; she perked up immediately. "Lance, you called; how are you?"

"Honey, I'm fine, but you probably haven't heard…there's been a fire and toxic emissions released at the refinery. I'm on my way down there now, and…"

"But, Lance, who's speaking for the refinery? You're not there, but who?"

"Well, as strange as it sounds, I'm the spokesman, taking calls from the media as I drive south."

"You're kidding, aren't you? You mean to tell me that the refinery has nobody there to talk to the media until you get there? That's ridiculous."

Somewhat irritated by her question—he didn't want to get into his disagreements with his boss about having a crisis-management plan—Lance responded, let me talk to you about that later. Let me hang up now so I can take any calls that might be coming through. I'll talk to you later when I get home."

Lance finally arrived at the refinery around six. Had he not known what had happened, he would have assumed everything was fine, normal. There was no fire, no fire trucks, no petroleum odors in the air. All appeared normal. He looked over to see Charley's office light still on and decided to go over there and get an update.

Charley was at his desk filling out forms, looking haggard and exhausted. "Charley, I just got in. Looks like things have settled down. You'd never know there was any kind of an upset here."

"Yeah, but believe me; it wasn't so calm around here earlier. I just talked to the Air District, and they gave us an 'all clear,' no toxic fumes in the neighborhood."

"Great. Another few questions regarding air violations here over the past five years, how many? And how many OSHA safety violations over the same period? Do you have that information?"

"As for the Air District, there have been a total of seven over the past five years, none, however, in the past year. For OSHA, just four. All were mostly violations for not following their rules. In those, the refinery has done fairly well, particularly in the past year or so. Not perfect, but still pretty good."

Lance could handle the lack of a crisis-management plan, but he really had no answer for the lack of a warning system for the neighborhood. He had never really thought of that being included in the plan. That could undoubtedly create a lot of community and council mistrust and loss of confidence toward the refinery. It could even move the council and the neighborhood to demand that the refinery close down. He didn't even want to contemplate such an action, but it could happen. He had two calls on his voice mail, one from Mayor Sims and the other from Roy Douglas, the neighborhood's activist. Neither was friendly; they were upset.

CHAPTER TWENTY-SIX

Knowing of his past issues with Douglas, he listened to his voice mail first. "OK, Mr. PR Man, I hear you guys over there just spread toxic fumes over the neighborhood, and you take damned near an hour to tell us to evacuate. You didn't tell us; the sheriff's department did, driving through the neighborhood with their foghorns blaring and scaring the living hell out of us. Many, including young children, were taken to the hospital. And I guess you bastards won't pay for that, either. Gimme a call; we need to talk."

Then he heard from Mayor Sims, who said, "Lance, you guys really screwed up over there. A big fire, toxic fumes spread all over the neighborhood, and no one called me or any of my council. We're not exactly chopped liver over here. I've had many calls left on my voice mail from angry neighbors. I'm serious when I tell you they want your refinery closed, closed 'til they have some kind of confidence that you know what you're doing there. Call me as soon as possible."

Lance took a deep breath, got his thoughts together, and called JB. JB heard the report, chuckling a bit when he heard that neighbors were going to force them to close. "Who in the hell do they think they are? Close the refinery? They can't be serious. As for those having to go to the hospital, we'll tell 'em we'll pay for that, but Charley tells me the Air District has given us an all clear. No toxic fumes to worry about.

I guess we oughta look at an early-warning system for the neighborhood so we can be ready if another upset takes place to affect them. That kind of makes sense, but we haven't had an upset like this one for years. So, Lance, go ahead and talk to that neighborhood creep who's been on your case about our operation here; try to calm him down. As for the mayor, I think he's OK, but go over there, hold his hand, give him the latest details on what's happening and what we plan to do."

It was now nearly nine in the morning; he'd start returning Douglas's and Sims's calls. He believed he had enough information now to deal with them, but he knew it wouldn't be easy. Their trust in the refinery and its operations had reached a low point. Responding to the two was not a task he looked forward to, but he had to do it. The combination of driving down from Sacramento, getting conversant with most of the facts covering the upset, and then being able to speak coherently to all the stakeholders had left him exhausted. And his day was now just beginning.

Since the fire had started around ten in the evening, it was doubtful whether the *Press Telegram's* coverage would have made the morning paper. Lance wasn't anxious to read it, knowing all the concerns the neighborhood and the mayor had with the refinery's lack of alert system regarding evacuation. He knew it certainly was not going to be a first-rate story praising the refinery.

Lance's cell rang again, bringing a look of relief. His caller ID indicated that Cindy was calling. He hadn't called her upon his return to the refinery, but she'd understand. In this case, dealing with the issue had to come first.

As he picked up the phone, Cindy started talking immediately. "Oh, Lance, you got home OK. I was worried. Everything all right?"

"Doing fine, love, but it's been a little crazy around here. The fire's out, no more toxic emissions, but the neighbors and the mayor are really pissed. They called late last evening. I haven't called 'em back. I was just about to do that when you called."

"Well, one good thing—the paper covering the fire won't be out until tomorrow. But the TV coverage has been brutal. They're not only covering the fire but also hearing the neighbors and the mayor really blasting you guys for not warning them of the dangerous toxins and telling them to evacuate. One of the stations even mentioned that the public-relations man was nowhere to be seen, and there was no person there to talk to them. I only watched two stations, but I would imagine they all had that negative slant."

"Not surprising. That's a typical way the media acts on an event like that. They have only a few facts initially, so they concentrate on our not talking to them. Hopefully, with the situation now under control, they'll emphasize that on the six-o'clock news."

"When will you be able to come over, Lance? I really need you."

"Can't tell right now, but you can bet as soon as I can get out of here, I'll be on my way to be with you. Gotta go now, doll; call ya later."

Lance felt the TV coverage she described could have been a lot worse, but he could foresee a blistering newscast and certainly a dreadful article in the next morning's paper. Oh, how he wished he was reporting on this incident as a newspaper reporter rather than giving its unrelenting and negative thrust to the refinery's missing spokesperson. Lance didn't want to be the main focus of the story, but without being prepared to have anyone there to speak for the refinery, he'd just have to take it.

CHAPTER TWENTY-SEVEN

Next on Lance's list was to call Mayor Sims's office and make an appointment. He could call him, but, under the circumstances, that would be unacceptable. A meeting was set for 2:00 p.m. that afternoon, and the secretary advised that there also would be two councilmen with the mayor.

Promptly at two, Lance arrived and met the mayor and Councilmen Rex Tate and Harvey Longacre. Looking at their collective faces, he knew they weren't there to talk about the pleasant spring weather. The evacuation caused by the toxic fumes wafting over the neighborhood was clearly on their minds.

Confidently and positively, Lance reviewed the situation, giving details about what had happened and trying to put an upbeat spin on the elimination of toxic emissions in their neighborhood. He told them they would do everything in their power to see that it wouldn't happen again. He was about to continue when Mayor Sims interrupted and yelled in a loud, animated voice, "OK, Lance, let's stop right there. What we want to know is why it took nearly an hour to warn the neighbors that there had to be an evacuation. You guys didn't tell us; the sheriff and his men had to drive around the neighborhood with bullhorns."

Lance recovered quickly and responded, "We called the sheriff, and he agreed that he would be the messenger. He felt that his men knew the neighborhood better than us. We were grateful for that decision and their quick response."

Tate took over the conversation, talking in a staccato-like style somewhat like a teletype machine, and said, "You see, I live in that neighborhood. We could hardly breathe; we were coughing. It was so bad, we went directly to the hospital. We thought we were going to die."

"I'm sorry about that, Mr. Tate. The refinery will pay for all of your and any others' medical bills caused by the bad air. The Air District has given us a clean bill of health; they tested the air after the fire was out and found that the air was free of any contaminants. For that, we are grateful, too."

Longacre, a tall, thin man with arms waving in all directions, joined the discussion. He stood up, faced Lance, and exploded in a series of expletives hardly suitable for a meeting with a mayor or anyone else. "Now, you listen, mister, lemme tell you what I'm gonna do, and the mayor and the council are with me. We're going to get the whole goddamned town over there at your stinkin' refinery and demand that you shut it down, shut it down 'til you have convinced us you know what you're doing and quit being a nuisance. We're sick and tired of you guys. Noises all the time, stinkin' out our good neighborhoods, not talkin' to us, and then chargin' those god-awful prices at the gas stations. Do you not have any shame? So, be prepared; we're comin' to get ya. We'll have the TV cameras there, the newspaper, the Bellflower Women's Club, and anybody else who'll want to join us. So, be ready."

Lance sat there speechless and dumfounded. He certainly didn't expect that kind of response from elected officials. This was supposed to be a meeting of civil conversation, one in which he would give the facts, apologize, and tell them that the refinery would commit to seeing that it wouldn't happen again.

Recovering, he replied in a soft, meaningful voice, "Your Honor, Councilmen, I do appreciate your frustration, your anger. I must admit we have not been the kind of neighbors you want living next to you. But that is changing; that will change even more. We've already made good progress with conducting refinery tours, planning to create a citizen advisory council, presenting our story to the chamber, other nonprofit groups here in town, being always available to respond to your calls in a factual, no-nonsense matter. Let's face it, no one needs or wants to live next to a nuisance and…"

Councilman Longacre interrupted again and yelled, "That's just PR talk, not worth your effort to even explain what you're going to do. That just doesn't cut it, mister, no way. You heard me; we don't believe you; we don't believe you can get your act together. As I told you, we're gonna have a huge demonstration right at the refinery's gate and demand you shut the place down 'til you correct your problems and promise no more. No more, Mr. PR Man. No more."

Lance had had enough of that man and his threats. He wanted to stand up, face him, and tell him exactly what he thought of this ridiculous talk. But he paused and quietly said,

"Thank you, Mr. Tate, Mr. Longacre, and Mayor Sims. You've heard me this afternoon, and now the ball's in our refinery's court. We intend to correct our problems and ask for your patience and indulgence while we do just that. Thank you for listening to me today. Good afternoon, gentlemen." He turned and abruptly left the room, much to the surprise of the mayor and councilmen.

Knowing that Pete was now back in the refinery, he called Lora and asked for an appointment. He explained that it was necessary for them to meet, along with Superintendent DeWitt. She got back to him immediately; they would see him now. Lance knew they weren't going to like his report of what had happened at the mayor's meeting. He knew, too, that they didn't want to hear about a threat of a huge neighborhood demonstration demanding the plant's closing, but he had to get it to them, unvarnished and to the point.

CHAPTER TWENTY-EIGHT

The boss looked rested after his family visit and had talked to his superintendent, who briefed him on what had happened, the outcome, and so forth. He was fairly relaxed with the report, but he was anxious to hear the results of Lance's meeting that afternoon. He anticipated the mayor and councilmen understanding and believed they would be reasonable about the situation and would support the refinery. He couldn't have been more wrong.

Lance gave a full briefing of the meeting. It went well until he relayed Councilman Longacre's threat to have the neighbors and the town's residents come to the refinery, demonstrate, and demand that it be closed. Pete went apoplectic, leaped from his chair, and started pacing the floor and filling the air with some well-chosen expletives that Lance had never heard before.

JB had mentioned the possible threat earlier to Pete, but both totally discounted it. There was just no way it would happen. They were sure of that.

"Lance, you're serious about this demonstration, aren't you?"

"Well, I'm just reporting what was told to me. Yes, I think it is serious; they seemed totally committed to it."

"No, Lance, it won't happen. They're not that stupid to do such a thing. We have too many of our employees living in the neighborhood. They'll come to our rescue; they'll set things straight. I'm sure of it."

"What we have to do is start discussing a contingency plan to deal with the possibilities. We'll need letters to the community, full-page ads in the newspaper, radio spots, person-to-person meetings with some of the movers and shakers in the town, the chamber, whoever." Lance was firmly convinced quick action was needed. His management better be too!

"All right, Lance, start doing that, but I wouldn't think you need to spend much time on it. JB and I will go over to the mayor and talk to him, ask him to cool it down. He certainly doesn't need that stuff in Bellflower."

"Right, I'll start it right now; we want to be prepared if it comes off. I believe you guys going over to city hall, pleading your case, should help us. It certainly didn't seem to do any good when I was there. But you guys are the top dogs here. They should listen to you."

Leaving the meeting, Lance had that sick feeling in his stomach once again. Pete still didn't quite get it; he thought that getting a plan together wouldn't be that necessary. The boss had had that same reluctance about having a crisis-management plan. Lance worried that they'd see the result of that when the TV and newspapers focused on the nonpresence of a spokesman at a refinery incident.

He knew then he had to call Douglas. He was sure Roy's complete wrath and disgust would come fully over the phone. After hearing the mayor's and council's threat, he was sure he and they had already discussed the demonstration and were ready to act. Lance was ready for it, but all he could do was listen and urge him not to support such a protest; he was sure his plea would go for naught.

Douglas answered his phone, recognizing Lance's caller ID, and said, "Well, well, well, you finally took some time from your busy schedule and called me. I so appreciate that, Lance; you shouldn't have been so quick to respond." The activist's sarcasm was expected, and Lance knew what he would hear next—neighborhood demonstration and so on.

He was not surprised as Douglas started word for word, complaining about the lack of early warning from the refinery, the toxic chemicals flooding the neighborhood, all of the same comments he'd heard at the previous meeting with the mayor.

"Oh, I hear you, Roy," Lance replied after listening. "I know you don't trust us, but we'll see that this situation doesn't happen again. We'll place a warning system immediately, and the Air District has given the all clear for the refinery. We're still investigating the cause, but for sure, we'll make damned sure it won't happen again."

"Yeah, I've heard all the crap before. Enough already. The demonstration is going ahead full steam whether you or your lousy management care or not."

"Thank you, Roy. You've made your position very clear. Just trust me, my friend; just trust me. Have a good day."

The call brought no surprises. Now, he had to start developing a contingency plan for the refinery to deal with the demonstration. He reported his findings to Pete and JB. Neither was surprised. "OK, Lance, get with it."

The evening news continued its negative report on the refinery's fire and delayed notification to the neighborhoods, citing its past safety and air-quality issues. Further, the refinery's lack of an on-the-scene spokesperson was noted. Lance had already called the major stations and provided an update on the incident, their investigation progress, and so on. He did the same for the newspapers.

The morning newspaper's report was relatively balanced; however, it did report that the neighborhood was planning a demonstration at the refinery to demand that it be closed until it could be confirmed that the refinery had its act together. Douglas's quote was especially harsh.

The paper's editorial, headlined with "Take No Prisoners," featured the community's disgust and impatience with the refinery, citing all the issues that were continuously causing an unacceptable nuisance. The refinery's workers were appalled at all that negative publicity; several of the foremen called Lance and offered their support to go into the neighborhood and talk to the neighbors. Lance appreciated that and told them he was putting together a plan to do what they had offered, in addition to newspaper ads and fliers.

Just after he had talked to one of the foremen, Bull Talbot called and yelled at Lance, saying, "What kind of PR man are you? You let TV and the newspaper make a fool out of this refinery. We've never been attacked like this, and now the goddamned neighborhood is going to demonstrate against us, and what are you doing? I guess taking another trip out of the refinery to do what, sun your sorry ass by the beach? You're disgusting, Lance. Simply disgusting. Pete is also disgusted with you. You should be fired and run out of here—sooner rather than later."

Lance could have briefed Bull on all he had done so far, including communicating with the media and keeping his management informed. He decided to say nothing to this antagonist. Some things are a better left alone rather than trying to explain. He finally responded, "Thanks, Bull. We're doing the best we can do; things will improve. Please be patient. I'll keep you informed as we move forward."

At that lack of a meaningful response, Bull became more antagonistic, more belligerent. In the middle of his tirade, with nothing else to say, Lance hung up the phone. He had had it with the man.

When the news of the refinery's fire and toxic release and its lack of quick response reached Bellflower's corporate management in Denver, Pete's general manager, Doug Jacobson, known to all as "Jake," called and was less than cordial. "What the hell are you doing over there? Why did this happen, and why didn't you have your PR man on the scene, or at least some kind of a mouthpiece there to talk to the media? The newscasts are saying there will be a protest demonstration. This is really disappointing, Pete, and I want you, whatever it takes, to stop that demonstration. Is that clear?"

"Jake, we feel the same way, but the PR man was out of town, and I had told him that we needed to have a substitute in case the media needed to talk. He started putting together a crisis-management plan but was called out of town with a family emergency. Unfortunately, he never trained and designated a substitute, and, well, you see, there was no one else here to talk."

"That's a flimsy-ass excuse, Pete. You, of all people, should know that the refinery always needs someone to talk to the media. I blame you, not the PR man. Whatever, I wanna see a plan in place immediately and certainly a few trained managers there to speak for the refinery, if needed. Clear?"

"Yes, sir, we're on it." Pete's boss was clearly upset. Pete now realized he should have listened to Lance, but since there had not been major incidents in many years, he just didn't believe he needed one, certainly not as a priority project. He was dead wrong and speculated that decision may well have cost him his job.

Pete called Lance and gave him the green light to start putting a crisis plan together, conduct media training, and implement all the ideas that he had previously submitted. He didn't want to tell Lance he was wrong, but whatever, the plan was now underway.

His superintendent was not privy to the conversation Pete had had with Jacobson. Pete called JB into the office, briefed him, and advised him that he had called Lance to implement the plan. "JB, I'm sure if we can't stop that demonstration, we're really going to be in trouble, both of us. I know Lance is putting together a contingency plan, but I believe we have to do something to stop it right now."

CHAPTER TWENTY-NINE

Hearing Pete's word to start putting together a crisis plan was a total surprise. Lance knew how adamant his boss had been about not developing such a plan. Something must have changed his mind. Perhaps it was the media's negative response to the lack of having a spokesperson on the scene. Perhaps Denver's management had read the paper, watched TV, and given him an ultimatum to put one together. Lance had already drafted a contingency plan, and now he would finish what he had previously started. He was going to be a busy man. He loved it. He was finally becoming credible with the refinery's senior management.

Meanwhile, Pete and JB met the next day and started thinking about what to do about the incoming demonstration. "As I told you, JB, Lance is putting together a contingency plan, but I believe that I've always had a good relationship with the mayor. Sims has been in office for five terms, as I recall. I'm sure in the next election, he'll be easily reelected, although my scouts tell me that the community has had enough of Sims and think it's time for him to go. I believe I can go over to his office, talk to him about the refinery's positive influence on Bellflower's economy, and ask him for some help to quell this demonstration. That's what I'm thinking."

"But, Pete, do you really think that just talking to him is gonna change his mind? Especially after hearing and reading his support for a demonstration, you think he's going to back down and try to tell the neighborhood to back off? I don't think so; I really don't."

"Well, I think it's worth a try. Maybe, just maybe, I can give him a deal he can't refuse."

"Wait just a minute. You're not thinking about giving him a bribe, are you? Please, Pete, forget that. You don't want to even give that a second thought. Think of something else. Maybe Lance's contingency plan will work, at least give us some support for the neighbors against us. But, please, no bribes."

"No, JB, I won't actually give him a bribe, but I can promise him that I can give him substantial financial support for his next election or perhaps one of his pet projects, whatever it is. You see, that's not a bribe; no actual money is being handed over. I'm much too smart to do that."

"OK, old friend, you're on your own. I'm just not comfortable with what you're thinking about doing. Good luck." JB got up and moved quickly to the doorway. As he left, Pete yelled, "Hold it, JB." It was too late. The superintendent had left the room.

Despite JB's decision not to approve Pete's plan, Pete was confident that he could pull it off. The mayor would be happy, the demonstration would be stopped, and peace and harmony would return to the neighborhood and the city. Pete was totally confident that his overture to the mayor would bring the desired results.

Pete's secretary made the appointment. The mayor would see him the next morning. Pete talked to Lanny Schwartz, his financial manager, and gleaned the positive economic information and benefits the refinery brought to the town with good-paying jobs, generous benefits, and so on. A closure would be devastating to the overall tax base of the city. Nobody would win in that scenario.

Now armed with the financial and employment information, Pete looked forward to the meeting. He had met and talked to the mayor many times during their presence in the city, but there were no personal relationships. Neither knew essentially anything personal about the other. Pete believed that worked to his benefit; he had never asked for favors. Neither had the mayor.

They greeted each other warmly. One would have thought they were long-lost bosom pals.

Off the bat, Pete offered sincere apologies for the recent incident. He gave the mayor a briefing of all the facts, reviewing what the refinery had done and would do to see that it wouldn't happen again. He was especially insistent that they would also make every effort to improve communications with the neighborhoods, keep them informed as to what was going on, and maintain an "open door" for policy issues.

"Pete, I hear you, and I appreciate that, but I'm afraid that it's a little too late. This past fire and release of toxic chemicals has become the last straw with the neighbors. You guys keep us in the dark time and time again when things happen over there that affect their lives; you guys just ignore us. That has to stop, and they, I, and my council believe the only way you're going to change is for us to demonstrate at the refinery's gate about the plant and our concerns. Understand?"

"But, Mayor, we are changing. Just give us a chance. Don't close us down; our refinery is essential to Bellflower's good economy. We offer good jobs, pay good salaries, and offer generous benefits. Please, Mayor, give us a break! Can't you do anything to stop this? Will you even try to talk to the neighbors and try to convince them that what they're doing is wrong, plainly wrong?"

"Well, Pete, I can try talking to Douglas and some of the other leaders. I'll really try to do the best I can, but I'm just afraid it won't do any good."

Pete waited a few seconds, as if thinking about what the mayor had just said, and then made his proposal. "Mayor, I know you're going to have a tough reelection campaign. Many feel you've been in the office entirely too long. I don't agree with that at all. You've been a good mayor for this city. You can count on the refinery to be a generous supporter with whatever money you'll think you need. Also, if you have a pet community project that you want to support, you can count on us to help lead the way with funding to make that happen."

Mayor Sims smiled and reached across and shook Pete's hand. "I think I know what you're saying. I'll think about it. Like I told you, I'll do the very best I can. Your promised support just might help it to happen. I appreciate your coming over this afternoon. Keep in touch."

Pete walked on air back to his car. He believed the offer would bring dividends to the refinery, and the mayor's influence would be enough to stop the demonstration. He couldn't wait to tell JB. He believed that JB would now believe that he had done the right thing. Things were going to get better.

He didn't tell Lance or anyone else what he had proposed to the mayor. He sure didn't need to have that spread over the refinery. The media might find out. He was sure that the mayor would keep the offer confidential. It was just an arrangement between him and the mayor; no one else would know or needed to know.

Pete's confidence was restored. He had been concerned that the refinery's fire, the lack of communications to the media, and a neighborhood demonstration to close the refinery would be the end of his career. Now, he thought he had taken the action to prevent that from happening. Some days were definitely better than others. This had been a good day.

CHAPTER THIRTY

Feverishly putting the pieces together for a demonstration contingency plan, Lance now had another task—to complete the earlier draft of a crisis-management plan for the refinery. It was almost six that evening. He was still at his desk when the phone rang; it was Cindy. He grabbed the phone like a branding iron and replied, "Why, hello there, my lady. How be you this fine evening?"

"I be fine, my lord, but your lady misses you madly. When are you going to get on your horse and ride over to my castle? I await you with undue passion."

Lance liked that and said, "I am putting away my troubles and will soon mount my steed and gallop in your direction. Please have your fire burning; my fire is now lit, and I shall bring with me a lovely bottle of cabernet for your pleasure."

"I can't wait for your arrival. Ride swiftly and safely."

Pushing aside the piles of paper on his desk, he rushed out to his car, made a flying stop at the grocery store for the wine, and drove straight to her apartment. All the stress of dealing with the upset and reading the media's negative report had drained him. He was almost brain-dead, but now he was revived by the thought of the evening with her ahead.

Bounding up the steps, now three at a time, Lance rang Cindy's buzzer. In a nanosecond, she came to the door dressed in a black negligee, her body shining through like a beacon of desire. He could hardly contain himself; he grabbed and kissed her passionately. "Are you ready for some good cab and a little Adele?"

"Oh my lord, you do know she's the very best. Just hearing her makes me tingle. Yes, I can wait, but, uh, not for long. I need your body."

The wine opened, now both fully disrobed, they lay quietly on the couch together and listened as Adele sang "Love Song" from her latest album.

> Whenever I'm alone with you
> You make me feel like I am home again
>
> Whenever I'm alone with you
> You make me feel like I am whole again
> Whenever I'm alone with you
> You make me feel like I am young again
>
> Whenever I'm alone with you
> You make me feel like I am fun again*

Taking a long sip of wine, Lance said, "I love that song, Cindy, just love it. It's exactly how I feel about you. I can't say it any better than the way she sings the words."

He had never told her he was in love with her, but he felt she knew it. Perhaps he should do that at this moment and get her response. His words came out so easily. "Cindy, I do love you. I can't say it more plainly than that. I really do."

"Oh, Lance, don't you think it's too early to say that? We've only known each other for such a short time; I believe we need more time. I know I do. The sex we've been having has been absolutely nothing short of fantastic. Smoking dope with you has been equally fantastic. In many ways, I'm sorry to ever have gotten you into that, but I did, and I think you enjoy it, too."

"Do I? But I gotta admit, if I'm going to smoke, I'll always do it in my apartment, your apartment, but I'll never drive stoned. Never. I would imagine if a cop ever stopped me, I'd be so wacko he wouldn't be able to understand me. But he'd sure know I was in no condition to drive."

"I agree completely. I almost always do it at home or at a friend's house. Never while driving. You saw me roll a joint in the car, but I didn't smoke it. I waited to get home and introduce you to its pleasure."

"You certainly did, my lady; now why don't we light one up, and you can continue teaching me a few more moves you learned in that incredible book, *Fifty Shades of Grey*. I'll continue to be a most apt pupil. You are teaching me very well."

And so another evening passed, with more incredible lovemaking, smoking dope, and wondering when Cindy would tell him how much she loved him. He naturally was disappointed she had made her intentions known to him. From there, he thought they could start planning their lives together. It never happened that evening.

*© Universal Music Publishing Group, BMG Rights Management

Cindy's phone rang. She greeted the call pleasantly and said before she began to talk, "Lance, it's one of my stringer friends. Wonder what she wants? Hello, Connie, what's up?"

Lance could not hear the conversation, but watching Cindy, he knew she was receiving surprising news. She finally spoke, "Are you kidding me, Connie? He did that? Unbelievable. It's going to be in tomorrow's paper? My friend, Lance, is certainly not going to like hearing this. He's here now, and I'll tell him when we hang up. Thanks, Connie, I really appreciate this. Good-bye."

"What's this all about, Cindy? What was your friend telling you?"

"Well, it's like this. Bellflower's mayor called the *Telegram* and said that the Bellflower refinery manager offered him a bribe to stop the neighborhood demonstration."

"He did what? You must be joking. Jess Peterson is not that big of a fool. He would never do something stupid like that. Never."

"I'm just telling you what Connie told me. Whatever, it's gonna hit the paper in the morning."

"Gotta go now, love; I've got to talk to Peterson and alert him to what's goin' on. I knew nothing about this; he didn't tell me. If he did what the newspaper prints, this will be devastating to the refinery and its future."

Cindy put her arms around Lance's slender neck and softly asked, "Anything I can do?"

"Nothing at this point; we just have to wait and see what plays out. This could be one helluva day," he yelled as he bounded down the stairs to his car. If he only knew!

CHAPTER THIRTY-ONE

Lance arrived at the refinery around six the next morning. The paper had not arrived, but as he entered his office, the phone jolted his morning's start. It was from one of the *Telegram's* reporters, Billy Masters, with whom Lance had had good relations.

"Mornin', Lance, I doubt if you've heard, but…"

"Yeah, Billy, I have heard. Haven't talked to Peterson. Doubtful whether he's even aware of what's going to be in the paper this morning, but…"

"OK, but we'll want to get a statement from you after you have talked. OK?"

"Got it. You can depend on it. I'll get back to you as soon as I can."

As usual, Pete was in his office at this early hour, reading his e-mail, on the phone talking to someone when Lance appeared at his door. Pete looked up, waved, and motioned for him to sit down as he whispered, "Just a minute; I'll be with you."

Putting down the phone, he quietly asked Lance, "What's on your mind? It's barely six. You're never this early around here."

"Pete, we have a problem. The paper's gonna release a story in this morning's edition that you offered a bribe to Mayor Sims to get him to call off the demonstration here and..."

Exploding with a series of harsh expletives, Pete yelled, "I did what? What in the blue blazes are they talking about? I did nothing of the kind. It's a bold-faced lie. All I did was offer him support for his reelection bid and, yes, for any community project that he wanted to support. Did I offer him money? Absolutely not. There was no money exchanged. Believe me, Lance, no money at all."

"I wish you had told me what you were planning to do. Don't you see? Your offer in the face of the future demonstration appeared to be made to get the mayor's influence and support to stop it. Was anybody else here at the refinery aware of what you planned to do?"

"Yeah, JB knew about it."

"What did he say? Was he for it?"

"Well, frankly, he was against it, didn't want anything to do with it, but I told him there was nothing wrong with what I planned—at least, I didn't think so."

"Look, Pete, I'm not gonna beat you up for this, but I wish you had told me. Like JB, I would have been absolutely against it. I'll prepare a statement for your approval and then get it out to the media, along with a heads-up to our managers and workers. We should also consider a press conference. I could handle that; however, they would want you to be the focus. I can brief you on how to handle it, but at this juncture, let's let it ride. I'll discuss it with Denver. Right now, we'll just go with a press statement.

"Again, whatever we or you say will probably not go down smoothly with the public, but we've got to get something out. By the way, I'm sure Denver knows nothing about it at this time. Do you wanna call your boss and give him a heads-up?"

"Hell no, I'm not gonna call Jake right now; I'll call him later."

"Pete, please. Please call him *now*. Jake needs to know. He doesn't like surprises, and a story like this will really rock him."

"I disagree. I'm the manager here, and I make the decision to talk to him when I want to talk."

At that point, Lance lost it, stood up, and faced his boss straight up. "OK, Pete, now let me renew the bidding on this. First, you're already in a heap of trouble with your reluctance not to have a crisis plan in place here. Now, you're being charged with bribing a city mayor. And you don't even want to tell your boss, your senior management in Denver? You're no fool, but believe me, listen to me, you're in a lot of trouble, not only with the community, but with your boss. Please do what I tell you. I'm your best support in all this, so for once, listen to me. You don't have the cards in your hand to win this game."

Now totally red-faced and with his forefinger pointed directly at Lance, Pete responded, "Now, you listen to me, you lowlife, know-it-all PR man; listen to me. You don't tell me to do anything. I'm your boss, and I don't have to do anything you tell me to do. Understand? Nothing. Now get the hell out of my office. This meeting is over."

Lance turned around smartly, walked out of the boss's office, and proceeded to write a statement covering the alleged bribe to the mayor. It basically denied the charge, indicating it was only a good-faith gesture to support the mayor in his reelection bid, and so on. Pete approved it with no comment or apology to Lance. With the statement in hand, he e-mailed it to the local media, the mayor and council, and Roy Douglas. He was sure there would be questions, but he would stand by what he had sent and hoped the story would only be around for one day. He knew that was wishful thinking, but what really worried him now was Denver's reaction. Pete didn't want them to be informed, but Lance was certain it would cause his boss more trouble than he needed.

Lance had had it; he didn't need all this stress and frustration in his life. He again pondered going back to being a newspaper reporter. Yes, there were challenges in reporting, but nothing like this. He then contemplated a decision that would probably be the end of his career at Bellflower—but as a professional, he needed to do it.

His phone started ringing off the hook as he received a myriad of calls brought on by the statement's release and the schedule for the press conference, if there was to be one. The media, as a starving lion, wanted to take a little hide out of the refinery's backside. As he had expected, the city and the neighbors wanted to close the refinery down in a barrage of calls that had Monica noting the caller's name, phone number, and so on. She walked into the office with her notes and said to Lance, "There's a real hurricane going on out there. Some of the language I've heard over the phone would even embarrass a sailor. It's really bad." As if Lance didn't know.

As the morning wore on, the newspapers hit the street and were delivered to the businesses and residents. There was shock spreading through the city. A bribe? What was the refinery manager thinking? The public demanded to hear from the refinery about the assertions made. They wanted details—full details, with no exceptions.

Lance finally made the decision to call Denver. He had nothing to lose. If he didn't, Pete would lose his job, and if he did, he'd lose his as well as Pete's. Whatever, there were definitely going to be some vacancies at Bellflower.

CHAPTER THIRTY-TWO

Denver was one hour ahead of the West Coast, so Lance deferred his call until nine o'clock his time. He had the public-relations manager's cell phone, and taking a deep breath, he made the call and waited to talk to Bob James.

"Why, hello, Lance Wilson, good hearing from you. What's cookin', Lance?" Lance had never met Bob James, only in phone conversations, although Bob was planning to get to Bellflower and meet Lance personally sometime soon.

"I hear you're doing a great job over there; at least, that's what one of my friends from Channel 10 tells me. I think your idea of having tours and developing a citizen's advisory council is a good one. I do know it's been kinda rough on you over there when you were not at the refinery when it had the fire and the chemical release, but that seems to have been taken care of. As you know, you guys have to have a trained spokesman for the media. Saying 'no comment' is no longer an option. So, hang in there, get your crisis plan written, have drills, and you're going to be all right."

Lance was amazed that James knew so much about what had been going on at Bellflower; he definitely hadn't been living in a cave there in Denver. The concern of talking to him about the alleged bribe had eased now. He was confident that he would understand and support him when he briefed him.

"Bob, I appreciate your kind remarks. Yes, we're making progress, but we have a long way to go to restore confidence in our city and its neighborhood. The reason I called is the article in today's paper and…"

"Article in the newspaper? What's that about? I haven't seen it. Tell me more."

Lance methodically reviewed what had been published, including the planned impending demonstration by the neighbors. He then had Monica scan the story and Lance's holding statement to be used to counter the charge.

"Oh, my, has Pete called Jake? If he did, he has said nothing to me. Did he?"

"That's why I'm calling you. I briefed Pete early this morning and strongly suggested that he let Jake know."

"What did that ole warhorse say to that?"

"Bob, he flatly refused to call him at that time, said he would call him later and…"

"Call him later? You aren't serious? The boss needed to know right then. You don't keep him in the dark with an assertion like that. You just don't. No one likes surprises, and I can damned well tell you, Jake certainly doesn't."

"Bob, I hate telling you this, but I felt I had to, if for no other reason than to give you an update about what has happened. Pete was adamant that Jake not be called until later, and I'm sure when he finds out that I called you, he'll be furious and will want to fire me. I really don't care at this point. I've done what I have to do."

"Lance, be assured Pete will never know about your calling me; I promise that. Believe me, all hell's gonna break loose when Jake hears about this and sees the newspaper. He'll call Pete immediately, and the conversation will not be pleasant."

When Bob James gave the news to his boss, Jack Jacobson, one could have heard the explosion all over Denver. Roaring like a wounded elephant, he said, "Frankly, I've just about had it with this guy. Yeah, he's been the manager over there for the past ten years. He has done a really good job, but lately, with the public-relations fiasco about the fire, the chemical release, the planned demonstration, and now this one, I believe that the man has just about, so to speak, 'outrun his blockers.' I just can't have this stuff happening over there. Refineries are not exactly the garden spot of the universe, but with the city and their neighbors upset, we must communicate—not later, but right then. Saying that, we certainly should never even consider giving city officials a bribe, even an alleged bribe to ask for a favor. I'm sorry, Bob, but we've gotta get him outta there. It's time for ole Pete to leave. I'll call him right now."

Lora, Pete's secretary, took Jake's call and announced, "Mr. Jacobson, he's away from the refinery just now. I'll call him and have him call you. Is it important that you speak to him?"

In a calm voice, attempting to disguise his anger, Jacobson replied, "Please do, Lora. I'd like to speak to him as soon as possible. The sooner the better. Thanks for your help."

In less than a minute or so, Pete was located and returned Jake's call, revealing no anxiety in his voice as to why his boss would be calling. "Hello, Jake, this is Pete. You called. What's up?"

After a long pause, Jacobson opened the conversation. "Pete, we've known each other a long time, so all I want to know, and I want it straight, is…what is this crap about a bribe you've given to Bellflower's mayor?"

Gulping, Pete answered, "Oh, that. Yeah, the mayor here went to the newspaper and…"

Jake interrupted, "Reported you had bribed him to get the upcoming demonstration stopped? Isn't that it?"

"Well, err, something like that. I haven't seen the newspaper, but, Jake, that's just not true."

"Don't you think, Pete, that you should have called me on this? What were you waiting for?"

"Yeah, I was going to, but…"

"But what? Did you think this thing was just going away, and I'd never know about it? Pete, this is the final straw with me. You just don't seem to get it. You don't understand the need for good public relations. You just can't run this refinery with your ever-lovin' head up your ass. You need to let me know what's going on there. That's your job as the plant manager. Pete, I'm sorry to tell you this, but I'm relieving you immediately."

"You are what? You are relieving me? You are firing me after all of the great things I've done over here, firing me because I'm doing a lousy public-relations job? Why don't you blame this PR guy we hired recently? He's the reason. I listen to him. He tells me what to do, and when I do it then you fire me."

"Now wait just a minute, Pete. You mean to tell me that he told you it wasn't important to have a designated spokesperson to talk to the media when he's gone, that he didn't tell you that you needed a crisis-management plan and to have some trained managers to deal with the media when he was away from the refinery? And he told you not to call me when it's being reported that you have offered a bribe to…"

"That's right, Pete; that's right. He's the one who should be fired and…"

"Hold it…one more time. You're telling me that all of the snafus that have happened over there are Lance Wilson's fault? I haven't talked to Wilson, but I just bet that for everything that he has suggested, he has documented and prepared some kind of memorandum, or an e-mail to you reviewing his position and your actions to either approve or disapprove. I'd bet on that."

Pete was not aware of such actions on Lance's part, but he knew he had lied to his boss; he had ignored the advice Lance had given him. "Jake, can we meet together on this? We need to meet face-to-face."

"No, Pete, I simply have lost confidence in you. You will be relieved immediately. I'll have HR prepare a letter to the refinery and…"

Pete interrupted and asked, "The letter won't give the reason why, will it?"

"No, it will simply say you are retiring after all your years," Jake explained. "Right now, we have to deal with the demonstration that's going to take place at the refinery. What are you doing about that?"

Pete replied quickly, "Well, Wilson has put together a contingency plan, and he's getting many of our operators who live in the city to go into the neighborhoods and…"

Jake asked, "When do you think it's going to happen?"

"Don't know, but I imagine the newspaper will know before we do. Maybe not."

In an impatient voice, Jake added, "Well, whatever, get the plan implemented as soon as possible. I think that's the way to deal with the demonstration, and if we're lucky, it'll never happen, and things will return to normal."

Agreeing with his boss, Pete said, "Yeah, I guess so. There's no one else here who has the experience to do that. Do you want to send one of your PR people over here to replace Wilson?"

"Don't believe that's necessary. The media and neighbors know Wilson; he's a familiar face, and I would think he'll be a good spokesperson for us."

"OK, Jake, I hope you're right, but I'd still like to talk to you face-to-face."

As far as Jake was concerned, he wanted to end the conversation. He ignored Pete's plea and without any emotion said, "HR will be contacting you immediately. Good-bye and good luck."

CHAPTER THIRTY-THREE

When Denver's HR manager, Ruth Sexton called Bellflower's HR manager, Sonia Thomas, Sonia literally hit the ceiling and asked, "What in the world was Jake Jacobson thinking? He can't do that. Pete Peterson's record here has been exemplary. He just can't do that."

"Hold it, Sonia; it's not a question of Pete's performance concerning the management of refinery operations; it's a question of Jake no longer having any confidence in Pete's ability to understand public relations. Now, with this bribe story hitting the media, this was more than Jake was able to take."

Sonia replied, "Well, I admit it's been pretty tense around here. With the paper now reporting that Pete gave the mayor a bribe to have him call off the neighborhood demonstration and…"

Sexton explained further, "Pete told Jake that he had not done any of the PR things because your man there, Lance Wilson, told him not to. As a suggestion, and please don't tell Wilson what Pete has said, go ask him to explain what his relationship with Pete was regarding public relations. He could at least set the record straight, and if Pete is lying, then that's a pretty good reason for letting him go."

Sonia agreed and said, "I'll do that, Ruth, but in the meantime, I'll start preparing a draft announcement regarding Pete's retirement. I'll get back to you."

Sonia was perplexed. Her relationship with Pete had always been sterling, only complete cooperation. She just couldn't believe that Pete had blamed Lance for the public-relations problems. Without calling, she walked over the Lance's office, caught his eye, and walked in.

"Oh, hi, Sonia, come on in. I was just wrapping up the contingency plan in the event the neighborhood's demonstration takes place. We'll have our operators here who live in that neighborhood go door-to-door and urge them not to demonstrate, tell them what the refinery does for the economy, good wages, benefits. I want that to start right away."

"That's great, Lance, but that's not why I'm here."

"Oh? What's on your mind?"

Without telling Lance about Pete's retirement, she asked softly, "Lance, when you offer a PR plan to Pete and he refuses to approve it, what would you usually do then?"

"Well, Sonia, as a former newspaper reporter, I always had the habit of keeping a log, a file, about what I had planned, and if my editors refused it, I would make a note of that. It's just what reporters do. As for here, I do the same thing." Lance then reviewed his past conversations with Pete and his refusal to approve a crisis-management plan, and particularly to not approve media training for selected managers.

"Hmmm, that's interesting, Lance. May I see your log or your notes on those instances?"

Still not aware specifically of what she was asking and why, he went to his computer, opened his crisis file, and called Sonia over to observe. "For instance, here's my notes on the crisis plan's discussions on three different occasions. See?"

Sonia sped through some of the entries and remarked, "I see. You have notes on all of your conversations."

"Yes, and here's the results of Charley and me talking to the railroad about their early-morning deliveries, disturbing the neighbors, and…"

Abruptly, she stood up, thanked Lance, and left. He sat there dumbfounded. Thinking out loud, he said, "What the hell was that all about? Why would HR bother to come over and look at my crisis file? What is going on?"

Sonia made a beeline back to her office and called Ruth Sexton. "Ruth, I just followed up on our phone call and went over to Wilson's office to see if he kept any kind of file on his conversations and decisions made by Pete. Yes, Wilson does keep one, and he has it on his computer's crisis file. I read some of the entries. It's very plain that Pete was the one who was making the decisions to not go along with Wilson's plan. It's very plain. If Pete told Jacobson that it was Wilson's fault, then Pete lied. That's more than enough to fire him, I'm so sorry to say. I'll start drafting the announcement for circulation not only to the refinery staff but to the media as well. Believe me; this will really shake people up around here. Pete's very popular, but they'll never know the real reason for the retirement. They might wonder about it, but they'll never know the real reason."

CHAPTER THIRTY-FOUR

The announcement about Pete's retirement hit the refinery and its workers like a ton of bricks.

Lance began to figure out why his HR person had visited his office and asked about his crisis file. He put two and two together. He thought that the PR problems had something to do with it. He wouldn't ask.

Again, he started thinking about his future as the refinery's public-relations manager. While he enjoyed the job despite its ups and downs, his real love was newspaper reporting. The experience in Lodi wasn't a good one, but there were a whole lot of newspapers around that could use his talent and skills. A whole lot. He'd have to give it more thought. He now had to focus on the potential demonstration that was bound to result in nationwide coverage. He and the refinery had to be ready for all possibilities.

The media started calling Lance to follow up on the announcement about Pete's retirement, trying to find the "real reason" for the retirement. Was he actually fired because of the recent public-relations snafus? Did he retire on his own? What?

Lance stayed on message and continued to state to them that Pete's retirement was just that—he wasn't being forced out, just retiring after more than thirty years with the company. Typical media, they didn't believe him and tried to seek other sources, but to the credit of the HR department, it, too, stuck to the script. The media's quest for further information soon ended after the first day of the news release.

He had gone to Pete to seek his approval for a holding statement, but to his surprise, Pete responded very tersely, "Lance, whatever you say, that's up to you. I'm retiring and have nothing more to say to that bunch of lowlifers. Nothing. Understand?"

"But, Pete, I…"

"You heard me, Lance. I am retiring. I have nothing to say to the media, to the mayor, no one else. I do want to speak to my managers. I'd like to do that as soon as possible, and I then want to get out of here. I have retired."

"Got it, Boss; I know they'll want to hear from you. You are really loved here. They're going to miss you."

"Oh, I guess so, but it's time to go. Anything new about the demonstration?"

"No news from that group. Roy Douglas is the main guy organizing that, but I haven't talked to him. I would imagine the demonstration is moving ahead. I have some of our foremen who live in the neighborhood organized to go door-to-door and try to change their minds. They'll be starting that when you approve it."

"Lance, whatever you put together. That's fine with me. I don't have to see your plan. It's fine with me."

"You don't want to see it? But…"

"One more time, Lance. No, I don't want to see anything you have in mind, your plans, nothing. Understand?"

"OK, Pete. I hear you."

Still at a loss as to Pete's sudden change, Lance thought he would call Roy and hopefully get an update on the demonstration. Knowing Roy, he felt he would at least get it straight from him.

He called late that afternoon and reached him immediately. "Hey, Roy, glad I caught you. Anything new about the demonstration?"

"Why, hello, Lance, funny that you just called. Me and some of my neighbors just read in the paper that that asshole who calls himself a manager has decided to retire. 'Bout time. We're all for that. It's time for him to go, sooner rather than later. It's good that it's effective immediately. Who's going to be the GM now?"

"I do not know who the new manager will be, but I can assure you, he's going to know exactly what the problems have been in the neighborhoods, and he'll do anything he can do to make it right. There's no other choice."

Roy responded with pleasure in his voice, "Lance, this isn't official, but after reading the news, I've talked to my people, and they believe with Peterson gone, we don't think we need to demonstrate. We believe that a new manager over there will start dealing with the neighborhoods the right way, telling us what's goin' on, making the refinery a neighbor instead of a nuisance. Lance, you've already started some things that make it better, like the tours, the citizens' council, and so on. So, we're going to call off the demonstration plan and put it to rest. We'll call the newspaper and the TV stations and tell 'em what we're going to do, and why we're doin' it. Whadda you think about that, Mr. PR Man?"

"What do I think? I think you just made my day, Roy. I can't tell you how much I appreciate that."

"I agree, Lance. We're going to look forward to working with him, with you and your managers. Stand by. The word's going out to the media."

Lance was ecstatic with the news. He was surprised that Pete's retirement would bring such a dramatic change from the neighbors. He just couldn't believe it. Lance rushed over and told Pete, and then the superintendent, JB, and of course, his corporate PR guy, Bob James.

Lance's call to James with the news was met enthusiastically. "Great news, Lance. I'll go tell Jake, and I can assure you, he'll be more than pleased. Great job. I gotta hand it to you, my friend; your work with the neighborhood has paid off big time. You've made the difference."

"Thank you, Bob. That's very kind of you. Frankly, I didn't think it would happen, but we were ready for it, had our workers who lived in the neighborhood going door-to-door, full-page ads, radio and TV spots. Soup to nuts, but such a demonstration, regardless, would really have been bad for our refinery and for the other refineries in the area."

Lance was so pleased with all the good news; he felt that his work at the refinery was finally beginning to bring dividends. It was his first public-relations job, and while there were serious issues, he was more than satisfied. His phone rang, and his excitement ended unexpectedly.

"Hello, Lance speaking."

"OK, big man, you've finally done it. Your mucking around with your fancy PR stuff finally brought one of my best friends, Pete Peterson, down. You did it. I just talked to Pete, and he gave me the full story as to why he retired. It was your goddamned fault. You caused it, you miserable piece of garbage. Listen here, and you listen well: I'm gonna come after you; just you wait. I'm comin' after you, so you'd better watch out."

Lance recovered from that onslaught of threats and ugly words and replied, "Sorry you feel that way, but now you listen, Bull. Getting a threat like you just gave me, you better think twice before you do anything. I'm reporting this to our people here, and I'll get a restraining order against you. You either cool your jets, or you're going to be in real trouble. You hear what I'm saying?"

"Now, don't threaten me, you miserable scumbag. Just watch out. I've warned you."

Lance hesitated to report what he had just heard from Bull. If he could see Bull face-to-face, he thought he could change his mind. He'd take that course of action rather than seek a restraining order.

CHAPTER THIRTY-FIVE

It was nearly six o'clock in the evening, and Lance was exhausted. Visibly shaken, he called Cindy and in an almost pleading voice said, "Cindy, I have to see you. I need to see you right away. I'm having a helluva day and just need a break."

"Gee, Lance, this must really be serious. Of course, come on over. I just heard of a new Italian restaurant called Luigi's. It's right off Capistrano Avenue. If we're hungry, uhhh, we can try it out. I'm anxious to see you. I need to talk to you, too, my love."

"Fine, Cindy, I'll drop by about six thirty." Paranoia crept in as Lance mused, "I wonder what she wants to talk to me about. Oh, well, after what I've been through today, there's nothing that is going to compare with that." He hadn't seen or heard from Cindy in almost two days—most unusual, since they either talked or saw each other every day.

She welcomed him tenderly with a passionate kiss, her lithe body pressing hard against him; his passion responded mightily. "Lance, you sounded really upset. What happened?"

Speaking in a slow, deliberate voice, he brought his lover up-to-date with all the bizarre things that had happened to him over the past two days. "Cindy, I've never been so scared in all my life. With this screwball maintenance manager—Bull is his name—making what sounded to me like a death threat, I'm at my wit's end. I decided not to report it to my people; instead I'll go over and see him face-to-face. I know he and I have more than a strained relationship, but when I tell him…"

"No, Lance, you've got to go over to HR and tell them. Whatever they decide to do or suggest you do, do it. Good gracious almighty, Lance, that's terrible. A threat like that can put the guy in jail. He's more than dangerous. He sounds to me like a psychopathic killer. As for the refinery manager retiring, wasn't that more than surprising? What's going on there?"

Knowing that Cindy was closely associated with the *Press Telegram* as a stringer, he hesitated to give her his idea of what had happened. He finally said, "Cindy, this is strictly confidential and only a guess on my part, but I believe he was fired for his ham-handling of the public relations at the refinery. Peterson essentially ignored almost every idea I offered him concerning PR. He even refused to tell his boss about the alleged bribe he offered to the mayor. I believe that became the final nail in the man's coffin. Again, that's only my opinion, so, for one more time, please keep it only between you and me."

Cindy quickly said, "Certainly. I won't tell anyone, but I think your opinion is very close to the actual facts of the matter. Do you think that's why this guy, Bull, became so infuriated with you?"

"I think Peterson might have told Bull the real story. Those two are longtime friends, beer-drinking buddies. When he heard the inside scoop, he didn't hesitate to threaten me." Lance wanted to share more details, like the HR person verifying that he had recorded all the plans he had suggested to Pete. At this point, he believed he had given Cindy enough information. It was interesting that she agreed with his opinion. Indeed, she was one very astute news reporter.

"Yes, and one more thing about Peterson. He's called a meeting tomorrow morning for all of his managers. They had previously received the news of his retirement, but this meeting is for him to say good-bye. He has already cleared out his desk and taken down all of his mementos from the wall. I'm sure he is leaving the refinery right after the meeting, packin' up and headin' for Texas."

Lance felt now the time was right to question Cindy, who had indicated that she wanted to talk to him about something. "You said you wanted to talk to me. What's up, my pet, what's up?" His lighthearted question was more than a veiled concern, believing she had something very important to tell him. Was she pregnant? Was she leaving the area? Was there another man in her life? He breathlessly waited to hear her.

"Lance, I really didn't want to tell you this. Whether you know it or not, I am in love with you. Our time together here has been more than special. Our sex has been nothing short of fantastic, and our getting stoned together has beaten anything I've ever experienced when I'm high. Being with you is such a hoot. You're intelligent, intellectually stimulating, and you're some kind of a lover."

Catching her breath, she went on and said, "Lance, you say you love me, and I love you, but I think I really need to let our relationship cool for a while. I just need to think about what might come next. I have mixed feelings about marriage, children."

Lance interrupted and said, "Hold it, Cindy. You know I love you, you love me, and we love each other. Why would you want our relationship to take a breather? It doesn't make sense. What's there to think about? The only thing we need to think about is our spending the rest of our lives together."

Lance paused for a few seconds and continued, "Meeting you and having you in my life has been the best thing that has ever happened to me. I love you. I want you, and I…"

Cindy interrupted, "I know, Lance; I know. But it's just the way I feel right now. I just need to you to give me more time. You see, I never imagined having a relationship like ours. Never. But it happened so fast. I have never been so happy, but I just need to wait and make sure. Please understand."

"Whoa now, Cindy, is it possible what you're saying is that our relationship has ended? Isn't that it? Understand, I'm on the thin-raggedly edge as to whether I'm either going to stay at the refinery or leave and get a job at a newspaper. I really haven't decided and…"

"No, darling, our relationship hasn't ended. I'm only saying I need more time. I have tried to explain that to you. Please try to understand."

"All right, my love, I believe what you've said, but, understand, I've got a lot of things to think about. You, my current issues with Bull, Pete's retirement, a new man to run the place, quitting the refinery, going back to a newspaper. I, too, need a little time. I think I'll drive back to Sacramento and visit with my parents. Up there, I'll have lots of time to clear my head and decide what I need to do. Bear with me, Cindy. Please."

"Well, Lance, having observed what you have done at Bellflower, I must say, I am really impressed. You are a natural. Frankly, I had never seen a first-rate PR person doing that job. As you know, I was never too positive about your being there, even questioned why you would even want to work there. But, having seen you in action, you have given me an entirely different view of how effective public relations can be at a refinery. If I were you, I'd give it your complete attention.

"As to going back to work as a reporter, I don't think you've ever heard me say this, but, Lance, stay right where you are. You're exactly in the right place for a long-term career, either here, at Denver, or wherever you decide to go."

Lance was astonished with Cindy's positive comments about Bellflower and a public-relations career. He answered, "Whoa, Cindy, I never expected to hear that from you. Never. But I guess your idea to let our relationship cool for a while is the right one. We need to clear our heads, and hopefully, we'll know what to do next. I'm going to Sacramento to give myself some quiet time to think about all of this. I'll give you a call in a few days."

As he drove away, he scolded himself for being so insensitive about Cindy's confession to him about her feelings. Further, her approval of him continuing a career in public relations was amazing. With all that had happened at Bellflower, he wondered if this was where he wanted to be at this juncture of his life. Were his education, training, and passion to become a newspaper reporter bringing him back to that profession, or was he just not facing reality? Going to Sacramento would let him step back and ponder his career and personal goals.

Clearing his mind, he now focused on hearing Peterson in the morning saying good-bye to his staff. Would the boss be generous in his praise for all, or would he specifically blame him for his retirement?

CHAPTER THIRTY-SIX

L ance was not happy about attending Peterson's farewell presentation, but he really had no choice. He knew he would see Bull there, and the last thing he needed was an ugly confrontation with that man. Maybe Bull wouldn't bring out his anger at the meeting, but he couldn't be sure. He'd take it one step at a time.

As the managers came into the conference room, the mood was somber. They chatted quietly, helped themselves to the coffee and rolls, and sat down. Pete's retirement was totally out of the blue. In their view, he should remain at Bellflower forever. These men and women literally worshipped the man. How would the boss address them? Lance wondered if Pete would even mention him. That was doubtful.

The HR manager, Sonia Thomas, gave a brief introduction summarizing Pete's career. Applause filled the room with each accomplishment noted.

Following her presentation, Pete was visibly moved and very upbeat throughout his remarks. He laughed and recalled many of the experiences he had had with the multitudes of managers and operators he had known and worked with over the years. His spirit became contagious to all. He thanked them profusely for their support and wished them well as he now moved into retirement. Lance listened intently, now confident that he would not be the focus of any negative comments.

As Pete was about to give his final remarks, he turned, faced Lance, and said, "Ladies and gentlemen, I want to say a few words about our public-relations man, Lance Wilson." The crowd grew very quiet. Only a few knew that there had been ongoing conflict between the two of them.

"Lemme be the first to say that as your Bellflower refinery manager, I really never had much use for public relations. My job was to run this place in the most profitable way I could. With your support, I am proud to say, we've done that pretty well. Our profits and our ROI have been impressive.

"But saying that, I essentially discounted most of the many suggestions that Lance Wilson ever gave me. His emphasis was always about the need to strengthen the refinery's relationships with our neighbors and the city. Let me confess to you, I didn't listen. I was wrong, totally wrong. Had I listened and approved the plans that Lance offered me, especially his idea that the refinery have a crisis-management plan, I wouldn't be saying good-bye to you at this moment. Retirement will be a relief from the stress of the past few days. Whatever, it is now time for me to go. Lance has truly been magnificent in his service to me, and with the new manager coming aboard, he damned well better listen. Thank you, Lance. You're the best."

As if the managers were programmed, they all stood and clapped. Lance couldn't believe what he had just heard. He simply could not believe it. As Pete left the room, the managers all shook his hand; many hugged him. It was a most moving moment. Lance had never felt so appreciated. It was a far cry from his reporter days at the *Desert Breeze.*

After standing aside and watching this memorable moment, Bull suddenly came over and approached Lance—his usual scowling face had turned warm and caring. "Lance, let me apologize to you. I just heard what Pete said about you. I was completely wrong about what you do and did in your position. Please accept my apologies. Anything I can do for you, whatever you need me to do, I'll gladly do it. I'll show you I know how to be a team player."

"Uhhh, thank you, Bull. I appreciate that. I have no hard feelings about you. I look forward to working with you in the future." Keeping the conversation lighthearted, Lance continued, "And keep my company car filled with Jet gasoline; it doesn't run on Chevron's or BP's gasoline, ya know."

Lance was, blown away upon first hearing Pete's laudatory comments and then receiving an apology from Bull. He mused silently and thought, *Maybe, just maybe, I might stay around here awhile. I just might have a career in this stuff. Maybe this is not the time to fold my tent and return to the newspaper business.* He'd make that decision while he took a break in Sacramento to check on his parents.

He and Pete were the last to leave the room. Lance walked over, hugged his boss, and thanked him for his most gracious remarks. "Pete, I really don't know what to say. Maybe I should have taken a different approach with you and..."

The boss interrupted, "Hey, Lance, forget it. I was just too much of an old-school guy. I guess I was still stuck in the nineteenth century. I remember the first time we met, I said to you when you complained about the odor here, 'It's the smell of money.' Do you remember that?"

"Oh, yes, and I have to admit to you, hearing that, I began to have grave doubts about ever taking the job here. Working here, however, dealing with the community, the council, the chamber, and the lame-brain railroad, I guess I got over it, but your remarks today will stick with me. For your information, I've thought a lot about leaving here and returning to a newspaper."

"Whoa now, Lance, please don't do that. You're needed here. You have really made a big difference. The neighbors respect you, the managers, the operators. Everyone you have met comes away with total respect for you. You don't always get that working for a newspaper. Don't you see, you are a complete natural for this business. The new man—his name is Skip Lawrence, an old friend of mine—will really need you. Please, dispel from your mind any idea about leaving. Please!"

Lance was surprised again hearing Pete's response about his public-relations success. Cindy's previous comments and now Pete's response were having a profound effect on the decision he needed to make. He still hadn't completely made up his mind about his future. It all depended on what century the new manager was in. If in the nineteenth, he wouldn't hesitate to leave. He didn't need any more of Pete's previous unwillingness to get with the program. If, however, the new manager's thinking and approach to public relations and community outreach was in the twenty-first, it just might make his decision much easier.

CHAPTER THIRTY-SEVEN

The transition period with the new refinery manager went very well. It seemed that Skip Lawrence had already been indoctrinated and conversant with public relations and its importance to the overall success of a refinery. He first directed Lance to finish drafting a crisis-management plan and directed his managers to undergo media training, lead tours, and involve themselves in the town's nonprofit organizations. He further requested and received approval to install the newest scrubber technology that would be significant in reducing refinery odors. The times were a-changin' in Bellflower.

Lance had already planned to get out of town and visit his parents in Sacramento. Both had recovered well from their accident. He felt, too, that a decision to return to newspaper reporting would be met with their complete approval, but he really had had no time to discuss his work at Bellflower. He decided not to mention his relationship with Cindy. He knew that his parents wanted their son to be married, but that would come at a later time. As far as his new fondness for marijuana, that certainly wouldn't be discussed. They would not be proud of their "little ram lamb."

Meanwhile, Cindy was essentially beside herself. She knew that Lance was more than upset with her decision to cool their relationship until she could get her head cleared and make the right decision. She had never been in such a quandary in her life. She was miserable. She knew Lance was on his way to Sacramento. He had called her just before he left. Their conversation was brief, somewhat emotionless. Both agreed to keep in touch.

She missed him so much, and as she relaxed on her couch, she listened once again to Adele's album, going through each of the many songs she and Lance had shared, talked about, and made love to. Their favorite was "Someone Like You." Its words moved her to sudden action and a decision.

Never mind, I'll find someone like you
I wish nothing but the best for you, too
Don't forget me, I beg, I remember you said
Sometimes it lasts in love, but sometimes it hurts instead, yeah.*

*© Lyrics @Universal Music Publishing Group, BMG Rights Management US. LLC

Cindy couldn't believe she had told Lance she wasn't ready for marriage. What was she thinking? Of course, she was in love with him; she knew him so well. It was time to clear her head and get real, get honest with herself. She rose from the couch, picked up her cell phone, and dialed Lance's number. As he answered, she said, "Lance, darling, this is your fair young maiden and lover. I didn't think I would ever tell you what to do, but, Mr. Public Relations Man, you listen to me. Any thoughts you were having about leaving Bellflower and goin' back to a newspaper, get 'em out of your head. You belong right here in Bellflower and with me. So right now, turn that car of yours around, and get back here. I want you now; I want you here and forever. I love you."

Lance almost drove off the road hearing Cindy's comments. He blinked and quickly replied in a somewhat stunned voice, "OK, I hear ya, and I'm comin' back. If I could fly, I'd be right over, but I can't do that. I'm almost to Bakersfield, but I sure as hell can drive almost as fast I could fly. We've got lots to talk about, lots! I love you. I'll be there as soon as I can."

Lance concentrated on driving and trying to read roadside signs. "Damn," he thought, "I really hate these California freeways. You spot an off-ramp sign but can't get over in the lanes to get to it." His frustration mounted when he realized he didn't have a clue about how far the next exit might be.

He drove over the speed limit whenever he could and usually had to slow down because of slower drivers. He made time and lost time, all the while wondering whether some highway patrol or unmarked police car would stop him for speeding, and he'd spend the night in jail waiting for a hearing the next morning. "That's all I'd need," he thought. Cindy would think he had changed his mind or that he wasn't coming at all. His mind was racing at Mach speed, out of control.

Then he spotted it! A sign showing a small turnaround, a one-way overpass. He knew he'd soon be home.

ABOUT THE AUTHOR

Gene Munger, a native of southeast Missouri, attended Southeast Missouri State College and received his BS degree in accounting in May 1956.

In January 1957, he attended the US Navy's Officer Candidate School in Newport, Rhode Island, and was commissioned as an ensign in the US Naval Reserve. He served on active duty as a staff officer with a NATO command, the Supreme Allied Commander Atlantic, Norfolk, Virginia.

Returning to civilian life in 1960, he rejoined Shell Oil Company and held supervisory and managerial assignments in retail marketing, real-estate development, mining ventures, and public affairs. He retired in 1991 as Shell's public-affairs manager for the West Coast.

After his retirement, he became a crisis communication and media consultant. In 1997, he moved to Flagstaff, Arizona, retired from consulting, and became fully engaged as a community activist and an author of four books. Those include *Momma, Don't Ya Want Me to Learn Nothin'?*, *The Elegant Mentor*, *Leaving New Madrid*, and *Return to Osage Beach*.

All royalties from his prior books and *The Smell of Money* go to his mother's endowed scholarship at Southeast Missouri State University. Shell Oil Company Foundation matches those royalties one-to-one.

About the Book

The Smell of Money focuses on a young news reporter, frustrated in his first job, who elects to take a position as a public-relations manager at a Los Angeles area refinery. This move brings instant criticism from his friends.

He had no training in public relations. However, soon after arriving in his new position, he becomes concerned about the refinery's environmental issues and lack of communication with the surrounding neighborhood. These concerns cause him to question whether he has made the right career decision.

Conflicts between the refinery manager and him about what is necessary to develop and implement an effective crisis-management plan solidify each person's philosophy. Ultimately, their differences highlight a series of issues that threaten to close down the refinery.

In the crisis-management role, the public-relations manager matures in his assignment, gains the respect of the neighborhood, city council, the chamber, and the media, and, in doing so, believes his new profession might override his long-held passion for journalism. He is torn between the two.

A torrid relationship with a local stringer for the newspaper adds spice to the novel and helps clarify where his future might be.

As a retired public-affairs manager for Shell Oil, author Munger's experience with his clients on the West Coast, particularly with its three refineries, was nothing like what occurs in the book. It is strictly fiction and in no way represents typical activities experienced by the author. In that connection, honest and open communications with surrounding neighborhoods and communities are the cardinal rule, never the exception. *The Smell of Money* reiterates these principles.